T0358247

Cambridge Elements ☰

Elements in International Relations
edited by
Jon C. W. Pevehouse
University of Wisconsin–Madison
Tanja A. Börzel
Freie Universität Berlin
Edward D. Mansfield
University of Pennsylvania

THE SELECTION AND TENURE OF FOREIGN MINISTERS AROUND THE WORLD

Hanna Bäck
Lund University

Alejandro Quiroz Flores
University of Essex

Jan Teorell
Stockholm University

CAMBRIDGE
UNIVERSITY PRESS

Shaftesbury Road, Cambridge CB2 8EA, United Kingdom

One Liberty Plaza, 20th Floor, New York, NY 10006, USA

477 Williamstown Road, Port Melbourne, VIC 3207, Australia

314–321, 3rd Floor, Plot 3, Splendor Forum, Jasola District Centre, New Delhi – 110025, India

103 Penang Road, #05–06/07, Visioncrest Commercial, Singapore 238467

Cambridge University Press is part of Cambridge University Press & Assessment, a department of the University of Cambridge.

We share the University's mission to contribute to society through the pursuit of education, learning and research at the highest international levels of excellence.

www.cambridge.org
Information on this title: www.cambridge.org/9781009475648

DOI: 10.1017/9781009441773

© Hanna Bäck, Alejandro Quiroz Flores and Jan Teorell 2024

When citing this work, please include a reference to the DOI 10.1017/9781009441773

First published 2024

A catalogue record for this publication is available from the British Library.

ISBN 978-1-009-47564-8 Hardback
ISBN 978-1-009-44181-0 Paperback
ISSN 2515-706X (online)
ISSN 2515-7302 (print)

The Selection and Tenure of Foreign Ministers Around the World

Elements in International Relations

DOI: 10.1017/9781009441773
First published online: February 2024

Hanna Bäck
Lund University

Alejandro Quiroz Flores
University of Essex

Jan Teorell
Stockholm University

Author for correspondence: Hanna Bäck, Hanna.back@svet.lu.se

Abstract: Foreign ministers are prominent actors in foreign affairs, often second only to heads of government in their influence. Yet, despite the growing awareness of the importance of key actors, and their backgrounds, in the study of international relations, foreign ministers remain understudied. In this Element, we make an important empirical contribution by presenting an original dataset on the personal and professional background of foreign ministers, spanning thirteen countries and more than 200 years. We use these data to answer three questions: who are the foreign ministers, why are foreign ministers with particular features appointed, and why do some foreign ministers have longer tenure than others? We find that foreign ministers tend to be men of politics who are appointed both on the basis of their affinity to, and to complement the experiences of, the head of government. We also find that foreign ministers stay longer in office when they perform well or are expected to do so, but that they are more likely to lose their posts when conditions make heads of government more prone to "pin blame" on them to deflect criticism from foreign policy failures.

Keywords: foreign ministers, secretaries of state, cabinet members, ministerial selection, tenure in office

ISBNs: 9781009475648 (HB), 9781009441810 (PB), 9781009441773 (OC)
ISSNs: 2515-706X (online), 2515-7302 (print)

Contents

1 Introduction

George Marshall was Secretary of State from 1947 to 1949, under President Harry S. Truman. In that time, he profoundly shaped US foreign policy, including, and famously, establishing the Marshall Plan, which helped rebuild Europe after the Second World War. Around the same time, Zhou Enlai was foreign minister of the People's Republic of China, negotiating with Marshall, and undoubtedly determining China's diplomatic and military activities for years. An early example of an influential European foreign minister was Charles-Maurice de Talleyrand, who was foreign minister of France during the late eighteenth and early nineteenth centuries. As Napoleon's chief diplomat, he clearly shaped Europe's history.

As these examples suggest, foreign ministers are prominent actors in foreign affairs, often second only to heads of government in their influence. Yet, despite the growing awareness of the importance of key individuals in the study of international relations and conflict, most previous comparative-historical research has focused on kings, presidents, and prime ministers (e.g., Goemans, Gleditsch and Chiozza 2009; Horowitz, Stam and Ellis 2015), but foreign ministers or secretaries of state remain understudied. This Element aims to fill this gap and thus focuses on foreign ministers as key actors.

The study of foreign ministers lies at the intersection of many subfields of political science. Foreign minister selection and retention speaks to the literature on cabinet formation, while also connecting to the literature of political leaders in international politics and foreign policy making, and clearly connects to the growing literature suggesting that the background features and experiences of political elites matter for their behavior (see Krcmaric, Nelson, and Andrew Roberts 2020). We draw on and contribute to these literatures here.

Our main contribution is empirical, introducing an original dataset on the personal and professional background of foreign ministers, spanning thirteen countries and more than 200 years. We use these data to answer three questions: Who are the foreign ministers? (Section 2). Why are foreign ministers with particular features appointed to office? (Section 3). And why do some foreign ministers have longer tenure than others? (Section 4). We argue that the answer to these questions matter for the content and consequences of foreign policy, and hence for the nature of international relations, but also for key characteristics of domestic politics, particularly concerning the nature of executive power.

In this section, we present a theoretical framework for the study of foreign ministers as key political actors within the international system. To understand why some individuals become and remain foreign ministers, we need to clarify what they can do – their function or roles. Foreign ministers have various responsibilities, which may vary across countries and over time. For example, in the US case, the duties of the Secretary of State include: serving "as the President's principal adviser on U.S. foreign policy," conducting negotiations relating to US foreign affairs, and negotiating, interpreting, and terminating treaties and agreements.[1] In the United Kingdom, the duties of the Secretary of State are described as having "overall responsibility for all Foreign, Commonwealth and Development Office business," including an "overarching responsibility for the departmental portfolio and oversight of the ministerial team."[2]

We argue that the responsibilities of foreign ministers or secretaries of state fall under three basic categories, with the foreign minister being an advisor, diplomat, and policy maker. These categories are not fully separable, and not all foreign ministers wear all three "hats." Nevertheless, these three roles constitute their primary function and guide our study. As *advisors*, foreign ministers occupy a key role as sources of information and arguments about the making of foreign policy. They make recommendations and provide expertise to leaders (be it kings, presidents, or prime ministers), who often rely heavily on their foreign ministers, and their primary function is to influence foreign policy decisions. As one of the highest-profile points of contact for foreign actors to the state, foreign ministers also serve a role as *diplomats*. Except for the head of state or government, the foreign minister is the most visible outward face of their country. In this capacity, they negotiate treaties and manage crises. It is principally a role in which they enact the will of the state, rather than one where they unilaterally make foreign policy, though that too may vary across regimes and contexts. Lastly, as *policy makers*, foreign ministers often have significant authority in and of themselves to steer foreign policy in a certain direction, by the making and enacting of foreign policy and diplomacy, including activities that range from crisis management or diplomatic recognition to the administration of embassies. In this position, foreign ministers can alter the day-to-day operations of the outward facing activities of the state, promote increases in the funding of their ministry, and, in some cases, restructure the ministry itself.

As should have become clear, we suggest that foreign ministers are key actors in international relations and in determining foreign policy outcomes, which other scholars have also argued. For example, Chrichlow (2005: 180) argues foreign ministers are "officially charged with directing foreign policy [. . .] foreign ministers typically have a great deal of discretion, and their institutional resources and authority, plus the legitimacy they possess as the government's

---

[1] www.state.gov/duties-of-the-secretary-of-state/.

[2] www.gov.uk/government/ministers/secretary-of-state-for-foreign-commonwealth-and-develop ment-affairs.

primary voice on foreign affairs, allow them to move policy in directions they favor." But we also argue that foreign ministers, as one particular type of cabinet member, provide an entry point for studying the larger issue of ministerial selection and deselection (e.g., Huber and Martinez-Gallardo 2008; Indridason and Kam 2008).

1.1 An Overview of the Literature

1.1.1 Research on the Role of Foreign Policy Leaders

We here draw on the literature which assumes that foreign policy outcomes are the result of human decision-making (Hudson 2005). Much work in this field focuses on the decision-making of political leaders, where several scholars have found that "the core psychological characteristics of presidents and prime ministers affect their personal policy preferences and the policies adopted by the states they lead" (Crichlow 2005: 179; also see Byman and Pollack 2001). For example, important work in this field by Hermann and colleagues (see e.g., Hermann 1980; Hermann and Hagan 1988; Hermann and Hermann 1989; Kaarbo and Hermann 1988; Kowert and Hermann 1997) argues convincingly that we need to focus on political leaders to understand foreign policy outcomes, and analyze whether and when the personal characteristics of political leaders influence foreign policy behavior.

We also clearly connect to the growing body of work, which in an overview article by Krcmaric, Nelson, Roberts (2020) has been described as the "new leader-centric research that moves beyond the earlier 'great man' approach or a general insistence that elites somehow matter," by instead making the claim that the "personal attributes and life experiences of individual leaders affect important political outcomes in systematic, predictable ways." The idea of this type of "personal biography approach," which we also adhere to, is that the characteristics and prior experiences of political elites have great importance for their behavior and the decisions they make (Krcmaric et al. 2020).

Several scholars have more recently gathered and analyzed comparative systematic data on the personal features of individual leaders. For example, Horowitz, Stam, and Ellis (2015: 12) present results that evaluate, on the basis of the background experience of 2,400 leaders (1875–2004), "the probability that a leader will engage in interstate military conflicts while in office." Later work shows that features such as combat and rebel experience affect leaders' dispute selection and the effectiveness of coercive threats (Horowitz et al. 2018). These scholars build on the important work of the creators of the *Archigos* dataset, focusing mainly on modes of leader entry and exit (Goemans, Gleditsch and Chiozza 2009).

Some of the conflict literature has focused on understanding leadership survival, since leaders' expected survival should influence their foreign policy decisions, such as their willingness to go to war or to make bargaining concessions (e.g., Bueno de Mesquita and Siverson 1995). This literature suggests that whether leaders wage war or agree to concessions depends on political institutions, with democratic leaders having a propensity to fight wars that they can win because victory in war is considered a public good, which is essential for survival in office in large coalition systems (Bueno de Mesquita et al. 2003). In terms of concessions, the logic of this argument is that leaders understand that concessions at the bargaining table could lead to peace, but also that such concessions could affect their survival as leaders. Therefore, the "size of the concessions he or she is willing to make depends on the sensitivity of his or her survival to the share of the pie obtained internationally" (Debs and Goemans 2010: 430).

Whereas some of these previous studies have argued that the postwar tenure of leaders in democratic regimes is more sensitive to war outcomes (see, e.g., Bueno de Mesquita et al. 2003), recent empirical analyses seem to suggest the opposite (see, e.g., Debs and Goemans 2010). Croco and Weeks (2016: 578) attempt to solve this "puzzle," suggesting that previous work has overlooked the leaders' "culpability" for a conflict. That is, when analyzing leaders' tenure and likelihood to survive, it is important to consider that the "domestic audience's willingness to sanction a leader" may vary both across countries and within countries over time. Here, a leader's perceived culpability for war is affected by whether the leader was in power when the war began. The degree to which a domestic audience is capable to punishing a leader also influences the leader's likelihood to survive in office. Another potential explanation for why democratic leaders do not lose their posts after a defeat in a war, also related to the argument about "culpability," is that other actors may be taking the blame for "poor performance" in such systems, such as foreign ministers, acting as policy makers or advisors of heads of governments. The underlying idea is that leaders can "shift blame" to other actors when losing a war, a point which we elaborate on in this Element. This kind of blame-shifting also has important implications for reputational theories of leaders and international politics (e.g., Wu and Wolford 2018).

There are thus several reasons for focusing on individual leaders when aiming to explain foreign policy outcomes. As mentioned, most studies have focused on heads of state or heads of government rather than on foreign ministers, which are the key actors that we analyze here. There have however been some important case studies on the decision-making of some influential secretaries of state which we can draw on. For example, Holsti (1970) performed an in-depth analysis of US Secretary of State John Foster Dulles' political beliefs, building on the operational code approach to the study of political leaders, arguing that key actors' beliefs and perceptions of the nature of politics and the world should influence their decision-making behavior. Analyzing writings of Dulles, Holsti (1970) presents an analysis of his political beliefs. Dulles' beliefs are then connected to his responses during ten international crises in the 1950s, for example, the Korean war, and the Suez invasion, suggesting that his view of the world and politics helps us understand important international events.

Even though such in-depth studies have given us much insight into foreign ministers as key actors, so far, there is little systematic comparative work that has focused on foreign ministers, and their appointment and personal characteristics. One important exception is the early work by Modelski (1970) that presents information on the background and "interactions" of the 175 foreign ministers who held office in 1965. Modelski, for example, shows that most of these individuals have a college or university education, often law and legal training, and that relatively few foreign ministers have military experience. Modelski (1970: 149) also shows that when it comes to occupational experience, many foreign ministers have a background in political office or within the party, but also that "the diplomatic service is another clear source of recruits."

Focusing specifically on foreign ministers and how long they survive in office in a comparative perspective, Quiroz Flores (2009) argues that affinity and loyalty toward a leader – particularly in autocracies – as well as the uncertainty brought about by leadership change and time dependence, strongly determine a foreign minister's tenure. Quiroz Flores and Smith (2011) formalize this argument, arguing that leaders face internal and external threats to their hold on power. Internal threats such as coups are more salient in autocracies and therefore autocrats remove high-performing cabinet ministers, as they are potential challengers to the leader.

1.1.2 Research on Advisors in Foreign Policy Making

A literature that we draw on focuses on the role of leaders and their advisors in foreign policy making. Scholars have long recognized that foreign policy is not carried out by leaders alone but that presidents and prime ministers often rely on political advisors (see, e.g., Hermann and Preston 1994; Preston 1991). Work on "decision units" also suggests that there may be circumstances when leaders choose to not exercise their authority. For example, Hermann (2001: 59) suggests that Franco in Spain turned much of his foreign policy-making authority to his foreign minister in the 1950s and 1960s. We here draw specifically on the work by Saunders (2017), who suggests, on the basis of principal-agent theory, that the balance of foreign policy experience among leaders and advisors affects decision-making in war. More specifically, she connects experience to the risk behavior of these actors and presents a framework where the imbalance in terms of experience between principal and advisor is central.

Giving examples from US politics, she suggests that George H.W. Bush was an experienced president who appointed an experienced advisor, representing the balanced, "controlled risk" situation. Franklin D. Roosevelt and John F. Kennedy were experienced presidents who instead reserved the key foreign policy role for themselves and appointed inexperienced foreign policy advisors, resulting in an imbalanced, "centralized risk" situation. An example of an "excess risk" situation, where an inexperienced president appoints experienced advisors, is George W. Bush, who appointed former commander and national security advisor Colin Powell as his Secretary of State. Lastly, an inexperienced president could appoint inexperienced advisors, resulting in a balanced, "incompetent risk" situation, with Donald Trump as an example, who appointed energy executive Rex Tillerson as his advisor (Saunders 2017).

Saunders (2017: 227) argues that the problem for the principal is how to take advantage of the agents' experience while avoiding problematic biases, and she identifies several mechanisms through which the leader can do so. One important mechanism, which she labels "delegation," is related to the idea that principals appoint secretaries with a specific background or expertise in order to be able to draw on the expertise and information of the agents. Here, Saunders (2017) suggests that when it comes to information acquisition, inexperienced leaders are better able to credibly delegate to experienced secretaries. This may also come with some problems, such as overconfidence and risky behavior among advisors, but it suggests that inexperienced leaders are more likely to appoint experienced advisors.

Saunders (2017: 224) also makes several important points about foreign policy expertise. She suggests that foreign policy expertise is "substantive expertise about particular foreign policy areas," and that experts are likely to be able to "use heuristics to assess which information is important, use their previous experience with patterns to make connections between pieces of information in ways that a novice could not, and gather and assess information more quickly and efficiently" (Saunders 2017: 224). Hence, foreign policy experience, of leaders and advisors, and the balance between them, is clearly important to account for when analyzing foreign policy making. Hence, such features may also matter for foreign minister selection, if we assume that those who select foreign ministers also care about which policies are implemented.

1.1.3 Research on Diplomacy in Conflict

As described by Quiroz Flores (2009: 118), foreign ministers are "the highest diplomats in government," and they "represent the sovereign state in one of its most important functions, that is, external relations." Hence, diplomacy is clearly a key function of foreign ministers, and we thus believe that it is important to draw on the literature on diplomacy in conflict.

But what do we mean by diplomacy? There are clearly many definitions of the term. In *A Guide to Diplomatic Practice*, Satow (1922: 1) defines diplomacy as "the application of intelligence and tact to the conduct of official relations between the governments of independent states." Sharp (1999: 37) describes a distinction between broad and narrow conceptions of diplomacy. He suggests that in the United States, a broad definition is often used, using it as a synonym for "statecraft, foreign policy, and international relations in general," referring, for example, to Henry Kissinger's (1994) *Diplomacy*. A narrow definition is exemplified by Nicolson's (1939) use of the *Oxford English Dictionary*, where diplomacy is described as "the management of international relations by negotiation; the method by which relations are adjusted and managed by ambassadors and envoys." Trager (2016: 206) argues that even though there is no commonly accepted definition of diplomacy, it is useful to distinguish "diplomacy from the management of foreign affairs generally," which is in line with our idea that foreign ministers can don different "hats," where the diplomat one is only one among three.

In a review article of the field, Trager (2016: 205) describes two broad traditions of scholarship in the literature on the diplomacy of conflict. The first tradition, the "diplomatic communication tradition[,] takes the difficulty of credible communication between adversaries as its central problem and analyzes the conditions for informative costly, costless, and inadvertent signals," and the impact of such signals on conflict processes. The second tradition, the "rhetorical-argumentative," focuses on rhetorical style and modes of discourse. Scholars in this tradition study aspects of the "style in which content is conveyed and the affective responses that result" and how "modes of discourse socialize actors" (Trager 2016: 207), referring to work by, for example, Mitzen (2005), Goddard (2009), and Risse (2000).

Trager himself belongs to the first tradition, which relies on the game theoretical literature on costly signaling (Fearon 1995; Morrow 1989). In the article "Diplomatic Calculus in Anarchy," Trager (2010) presents a bargaining model showing that diplomatic communication can affect the likelihood of conflict, particularly when the actors involved value their reputations. When communication can alter how one actor perceives the intentions of another, it is used more carefully, if the actor realizes that communication comes with a cost. Crucially, the actor communicating needs to understand that threats will affect how other actors view their intentions. If the actor making the threat does not understand that threats affect perceptions, they will not be able to communicate effectively.

Another piece of work that is important to mention here is Neumann's (2012) *At Home with the Diplomats*, which builds on an ethnographic study of the inner workings of a foreign ministry. Neumann shows that there are differences between diplomats working "at home" and diplomats working "in the field" in what activities they are mainly engaged with. Diplomats in the field, working abroad, are mainly engaged in gathering and processing information, whereas diplomats working in their home capital are mainly engaged in producing various texts, such as reports or speeches. A main argument of Neumann (2012) is that foreign ministries focus mainly on the internal process of finding agreement among various departments than on the purpose and audience of a specific speech or a text, suggesting that diplomatic professionals are "conformists," who do not exercise much agency of their own.

1.1.4 The Comparative Literature on Ministerial Selection and Deselection

Since we are specifically focusing on why certain individuals become and stay foreign ministers, we also draw on the comparative literature on the "hiring and firing" of cabinet ministers more generally. This literature departs from a view of democracies as based upon a chain of delegation in which the head of government (HoG) acts as "principal" of the ministers who are acting as "agents." According to principal-agent theory, the principal employs several control mechanisms to mitigate "agency loss," that is, to avoid that the ministers act against the wishes of the HoG.

Kam, Bianco, Sened, and Smyth (2010: 1) ask, How can the principal ensure that the line ministers act in accordance with his or her wishes? One answer is to select those individuals for cabinet whose policy preferences are as close as possible to the principal's own preferences. Focusing on the United Kingdom, the key question they ask is who the principal is in the ministerial appointment process: the party leader or the backbenchers. Building on this work, Bäck, Debus, and Müller (2016) argue that there are three potentially dominant principals in ministerial selection in coalition governments: the party, the prime minister (PM), and the coalition as a collective. Which principal is dominant, they argue, depends on the institutional setting, and a main conclusion is that politicians are appointed to cabinet if they are ideologically close to the dominant principal, in order to limit agency loss.

Relevant to our analyses of foreign ministers are studies of the appointment of "technocrats." For example, Amorim Neto and Strøm (2006) discuss how appointments of nonpartisan ministers – often associated with skilled technocrats or experts – signal that "efficiency concerns" trump "redistributive ambitions." In a similar vein, Hallerberg and Wehner (2020) argue that certain backgrounds will be more likely among ministers appointed during times of economic crisis. Governments in an economic crisis need to gain the confidence of both investors and of voters, and the appointment of a "technically competent" minister may help the government gain credibility (Hallerberg and Wehner 2020: 8; see also Alexiadou and Gunaydin 2019).

While extensive "screening" is the most important *ex ante* measure to avoid agency loss arising from delegation, the most important *ex post* measure is the ability to simply remove the agents. Thus, the opportunity to dismiss ministers deemed incompetent, disloyal, or exceeding their range of discretion is typically characterized as an effective sanctioning instrument for the PM, who is typically portrayed as the main principal in this literature (e.g., Huber and Martinez-Gallardo 2008). There is a growing literature focusing on explaining why certain ministers stay longer in their posts while others are removed from their posts. This work views cabinet reshuffles and ministerial dismissals as means to limit agency loss. Dismissals may, for example, mitigate adverse selection problems by "re-matching" portfolio and talents or weeding out of "bad" ministers (see, e.g., Indridason and Kam 2008).

1.2 A Theoretical Framework: Foreign Ministers as Agents

We are now positioned to outline a framework for theorizing about why some individuals become foreign ministers and why some stay longer in this office. Our theoretical expectations are based on a principal-agent framework, building on arguments made in the comparative literature on ministerial selection and deselection described earlier. Hence, we conceive of the relationship between the HoG and his or her foreign ministers as one of principal and agent. According to principal-agent theory, the HoG as principal employs several control mechanisms to mitigate "agency loss," that is, to avoid that the ministers act against the wishes of the HoG. A main control mechanism to avoid agency loss is to extensively screen potential candidates for cabinet (e.g., Strøm 2003), and through careful selection "work to ensure that their ministers [. . .] are behaving as faithful agents behind closed doors of the cabinet office" (Kam et al. 2010: 1).

We are here interested in the personnel decisions made by HoGs. Hence, we should take our starting point in the goals of these leaders. Following the previous literature, HoGs (prime ministers, presidents, kings, etc.) are assumed to be primarily interested in staying in office. In democratic systems this implies that they are instrumentally vote-seeking; that is, they should to some extent aim to "please their voters." In addition, leaders in any regime may also be policy-seeking in the sense that they are interested in implementing a specific policy program in order to remain in office (Bueno de Mesquita et al. 2003). For office-, policy-, or vote-seeking reasons, leaders should thus be interested in hiring and keeping high-performing ministers, and should aim to make personnel decisions that minimize agency loss.

However, as has been noted in the literature on ministerial selection and survival, HoGs are not always free to staff the cabinet as they see fit, without the approval of some other actors. Comparative research also shows that the risk that a minister gets fired is lower in coalition governments, suggesting that the prime minister is constrained when making personnel decisions in such cabinets (Huber and Martinez-Gallardo 2008). Hence, even if we restrict ourselves to parliamentary democracies, it is not always clear that the PM is the main principal in the ministerial appointment process, and ministers in coalition governments may clearly have competing principals (e.g., Bäck et al. 2016). The literature on decision units and foreign policy making make similar claims. Here, scholars have suggested that it is important to consider that some governments are characterized by a "sharp fragmentation of political authority within the decision unit," arguing that any actor may be able to block initiatives of the other actors, for example, by threatening to leave, thereby bringing the cabinet down (Hagan et al. 2001: 170).

Hence, it is clearly a simplification to say that the HoG is always making decisions about ministers' appointment and tenure. Even though reality is more complex, we believe that when it comes to the hiring and firing of foreign ministers, other actors – such as the party or the ruling coalition undergirding a leader's tenure in office in more personalized dictatorships (Svolik 2012) – should have similar interests as the HoG; that is, they are likely to appreciate and reward positive performance, and to depreciate and punish poor performance.

We suggest that HoGs will try to evaluate *ex ante* performance of potential ministers, which should be determined by the individual background features of foreign ministers, but they may also evaluate *ex post* performance, which is likely to be determined by situational features such as the level and outcomes of conflicts that the country is involved in. As argued by Quiroz Flores and Smith (2011), new ministers, by definition, have not revealed their level of performance – competence or performance, however defined or measured, is an unknown quantity. Yet, some ministers are more experienced than others: all else equal, ministers with a long career in the diplomatic service are, for example, expected to perform better during international conflicts than ministers without any diplomatic experience. In this light, *expected* performance keeps ministers in office, at least until a sufficient quantity of actual performance is observed. However, foreign ministers may also be blamed or rewarded for the situation that the country is in. In other words, we refer to *actual* performance and the *perception* it produces about a minister's competence.

We center on foreign minister *experience* in our argument, with professional background as both the source of and our measurement for experience. Experience brings expertise, which have a variety of implications for decision-making and job performance. We highlight three types of expertise in particular: diplomatic expertise, political expertise, and foreign policy expertise. Each captures a particular skill set, but may – and frequently do – overlap. Experience can change how other actors, particularly leaders, relate to foreign ministers. For example, experience may cause leaders to be more deferential to the foreign minister, changing the nature of the principal-agent relationship. Experience can also make a foreign minister more competent at specialized aspects of their job, distinct from the manner in which they process information and make decisions.

We suggest that one important type of expertise for foreign ministers is *diplomatic* expertise. Ministers with this background – for example, gained through experience as diplomats – are likely to be more skillful negotiators. They are likely to be better communicators in the international arena. In other words, they are better at being the face of the state in international negotiations, because they are more experienced at it. Previous diplomatic experience may familiarize a foreign minister with peculiarities in diplomatic communication or process. That familiarity may increase their competence in some tasks, and we thus suggest that this type of experience is important to account for when aiming to answer questions about who is selected to be foreign minister and why some ministers have longer tenure.

1.3 Data on Foreign Ministers

This Element draws on a unique and newly constructed dataset covering foreign ministers or secretaries of state in thirteen former or current great powers. Through a team of research assistants knowledgeable in the language of the country they coded, we have collected biographical information on over 1,100 regular foreign-minister terms from the selected countries, including information on the personal backgrounds of foreign ministers before entering office.

The thirteen included countries are: Austria (the Habsburg Empire/Austria-Hungary), Britain, China (Qing Empire/Republic/People's Republic of China),

France, Italy, Japan, the Netherlands, the Ottoman Empire/Turkey, Prussia/ Germany, Russia/USSR, Spain, Sweden, and the United States. Although our data only cover the post-1789 period, we thus include all thirteen great powers in the international system from the early modern period to the present (Levy 1983). Apart from the fact that we are capturing the most influential foreign ministers in modern times, this sample provides variation across countries and over time in regime characteristics and conflict propensity. Although it would certainly have been interesting to also include recently emerging powers such as India, Mexico, or Brazil, we leave that for future research.

It should be made clear at the outset that while our data spans more than two centuries, in which enormous development has occurred both in terms of how states are being governed and the nature of international relations, our approach in this Element is, by and large, to abstract away from the time- or period-specific to the more general. One could have argued with Buzan and Lawson (2014), for example, that at particular "benchmark dates" during the long period under study in this Element, such as 1860 or 1942, one should have expected a structural change in the relationship determining who becomes appointed as foreign minister or how long they remain in office. Similarly, we agree with Leira (2019) that the concept of "foreign policy" as such is not given by nature but changes throughout the course of history. What we will be able to present within the limits of this Element, however, are only the underlying explanatory patterns stable enough to affect foreign minister appointments and dismissals *despite* recurrent change in the surrounding context. Studying such interactions between time periods or historical eras and these more structural causes is another topic highly worthy of future study.

1.4 Outline and Preview of Empirical Findings

Section 2 presents our historical data collection and presents the background features of the foreign ministers whom we study in a descriptive manner. In line with Modelski (1970), we find that the majority of foreign ministers lack military background. Perhaps somewhat surprisingly, foreign ministers overall have predominantly *not* had personal experience with diplomatic service abroad. In terms of political experience more generally, foreign ministers are clearly no rookies. When counting membership in a political party or background in a legislature, in the cabinet or other higher government office, only 10 percent of the foreign ministers in our sample lack any such experience.

Section 3 of the Element focuses on the appointment of foreign ministers, and the question of whether it matters that they have a specific background and who the leader of the cabinet is. Drawing on the theoretical framework described earlier, we hypothesize that politicians with similar backgrounds to their leaders are more likely to become foreign ministers, since leaders expect that such ministers will have similar preferences to their own. We also hypothesize that politicians who are experienced foreign policy makers (diplomats), or have a military background, will be appointed when the country faces a geopolitical threat. The results, for example, show that leaders with a military background are more likely to appoint foreign ministers with a similar background, supporting the idea that "affinity" is important for leaders to limit agency loss. We also find that experienced leaders, who have long been in office, are less likely to appoint experienced foreign ministers.

Section 4 focuses on the ministers' tenure, and the question of why some foreign ministers sit longer on their posts than others. We contribute to the literature by evaluating original hypotheses about the features that influence foreign ministerial survival. We expect that specific background features of the individual ministers influence their tenure, for example, hypothesizing that foreign ministers with a diplomatic background have a lower risk of losing their posts because they are expected to perform well in office. We also hypothesize that the survival of foreign ministers depends on situational features, and that foreign ministers are less likely to survive after a loss of war, either because this can be perceived as a "poor performance" on their part or because heads of governments will shift blame within cabinet to avoid losing office.

Analyzing our data on foreign ministers, we find several performance-related features that matter for foreign minister tenure. First, diplomatic experience decreases the likelihood of forced resignation, suggesting that some foreign ministers stay in office due to an expected high performance. Just as in some of the previous literature on leadership survival (see, e.g., Bueno de Mesquita and Siverson 1995), we find that conflict matters for foreign minister tenure. Second, we find support for the hypothesis that foreign ministers are significantly more at risk of losing their posts if the level of conflict is high during his or her time in office. We argue that the most likely mechanism underlying this is that HoGs "pin blame" on individual ministers and deflect criticism by removing the foreign minister when the country is involved in a conflict. We also find support for the idea that positive conflict outcomes, such as winning a conflict or ending it by reaching a compromise agreement, increases the foreign ministers' tenure, suggesting that "good performance" is rewarded.

Section 5 summarizes our findings in the empirical sections and draws attention back to the key roles of foreign ministers, as advisors, diplomats, and policy makers. We here discuss potential implications of our findings about who becomes foreign minister and what explains their tenure for foreign policy making, such as for conflict escalation and state recognition. Hence, we suggest how our comparative-historical data on the background and exits of foreign ministers can be used in future research on international relations and foreign policy making, as well as for the future comparative study of ministerial selection and deselection.

2 Foreign Ministers since 1789

Who becomes foreign minister? What background characteristics have been typical among the people holding this prestigious post since the time of the French Revolution? How long does a foreign minister typically stay in office? And through what processes do they leave?

To answer these questions, this Element draws on a unique and newly constructed dataset covering foreign ministers, or secretaries of state, in thirteen former or current great powers since 1789. The countries included are, to begin with, Austria, until 1866 called the Habsburg Empire and from 1867 to 1918 Austria-Hungary (or the Double Monarchy), a great power since medieval times that lost this status after the First World War. Second, China, until 1911 called the Qing Empire, from 1911 to 1948 the Republic of China, and since 1949, when it achieved great power status, the People's Republic of China. Third, France, one of the first great powers in the world system, and still remaining one. Fourth, Germany, which we upon unification in 1870 treat as a continuation of Prussia, a country that achieved great power status already in the eighteenth century, and since 1940 called the German Federal Republic (thus excluding East Germany). Fifth, Italy, a country that became a great power upon unification in 1860 but lost that status during the Second World War. Sixth, Japan, considered a great power after winning the first Sino-Japanese war over China in 1895, but – like Italy – lost that status in the Second World War. Seventh and eighth, the Netherlands and Sweden, two seventeenth-century great powers declining from the scene of great power politics already in the eighteenth century. Ninth, Russia, between 1922 and 1991 called the Union of Soviet Socialist Republics, or USSR, a great power since the early eighteenth century. Tenth, Spain, also among the earliest medieval great powers that lost this status during the Napoleonic wars. Eleventh, Turkey, until 1922 called the Ottoman Empire, which achieved great power status in medieval times but lost it already in the seventeenth century. Twelfth, the United Kingdom, a long-standing and remaining great power. Thirteenth, finally, the United States of America, usually considered a great power since winning the Spanish-American war in 1898.

Although our data only cover the post-1789 period, these thirteen states comprise the full set of great powers in the international system from the early modern period to the present (Levy 1983). Apart from the fact that we are thus arguably capturing the most influential foreign ministers in modern times, this sample of countries also provides ample variation both across countries and over time in terms of political regimes. All of these current or former great powers – with the clear exceptions of China and Russia, and more recently also Turkey – are today close to fully developed electoral democracies. However, this was, of course, not the case historically. By the end of the nineteenth century, only France, the Netherlands, Sweden, the United Kingdom and the United States had something akin to a fledgling half-grown electoral democracy, and even in those countries there were still large limitations in terms of the extension of the suffrage and the freedom and fairness of elections (among other things). Moreover, even among the more fully developed electoral democracies of today, Italy, Germany and Austria experienced serious setbacks in the mid-war period, Spain from the late 1930s until the mid-1970s, whereas Japan only democratized after the Second World War. This variation matters since, as we shall see, the logic of both foreign minister appointment and dismissal varies across regime types.

2.1 Defining Foreign Ministers

The starting point of our data collection for each of these countries, if later than 1789, depends on what the term "foreign minister" more exactly is interpreted to mean. A broad definition would be the highest official in a country or state "exclusively or at least mainly concerned with the formulation and carrying-out of foreign policy" (Anderson 1993: 73). This definition, however, leaves two problems unresolved. The first is how functionally differentiated the role of foreign minister must be from other government posts, most importantly the one as head of state or HoG. The nineteenth-century German statesman Otto von Bismarck is here a case in point, simultaneously holding the position as Reichskanzler (under the German Emperor) and Prussian Minister of Foreign Affairs, the latter de facto implying foreign minister for the whole of Germany. Since Bismarck fused the two roles, his case raises the question of how functionally differentiated you have to be to be considered a foreign minister as such, and not just a HoG (or head of state). Second, how much policy-making authority must a foreign minister have to count as such? Purely administrative personnel that only carry out the decisions of rulers higher in the hierarchy should obviously be excluded, but where to draw the line? To refer to another example from Imperial Germany, the "state secretaries," who formally headed the foreign office but in practice were subordinate to the chancellors (Doss 1982: 230), are a case in point. Are they to be considered foreign ministers?

Our solution to both these problems is to operationally only consider a foreign minister as such if he or she (a) holds such a title (possibly together with other titles) and (b) presides over a ministry of foreign affairs. This would seem to ensure both a minimal level of functional differentiation and policy-making authority. As a consequence, Bismarck and all other German chancellors up until the fall of Imperial Germany in 1918 except one[3] are considered Germany's foreign ministers, whereas the "state secretaries" are excluded on account of not holding the title. By the same criteria, Russia/USSR enters our series in 1802 with the establishment of the Imperial Ministry of Foreign Affairs, preceded over by a minister (Uldricks 1982: 517); Sweden in 1809, when the title of "State Minister for Foreign Affairs" was first introduced (Carlgren 1982: 458); the Netherlands in 1814 (Wels 1982: 366–368); Italy upon its unification in 1861 (Serra 1982: 298); the Ottoman Empire with the first creation of a foreign ministry in 1836 (Kuneralp 1982: 500); China (then the Qing Empire) upon the same in 1861 (Hsu 1982: 122–124); followed by Japan in 1868 (Nish 1982: 328).

The United Kingdom, the United States, France, and Spain present no special problems in terms of finding a starting date, all having foreign ministers (or "secretaries of state") by title and in charge of a foreign office since our starting year in 1789 (Cromwell 1982; De Santis and Heinrichs 1982; Dethan 1982; Smyth 1982).

The Austrian Empire presents a borderline case: although a ministry of foreign affairs was not established until 1848, Clemens von Metternich had held the title of foreign minister since 1809, together with that of state chancellor since 1821. Since the function of the State Chancery he presided over was *not* only to formulate foreign policy (Rumpler 1982: 52), one could have argued, by the lack of functional differentiation from other government positions, that Metternich should have been excluded from our sample. Being the architect of the European international system after the congress of Vienna up until the revolutions of 1848, when he finally lost office, Metternich is, however, considered one of the most influential foreign ministers of all times. We have therefore decided to include him.[4]

In all cases, our data includes all foreign ministers up until May 2017, when our data collection ended. Excluding those who were only acting for the actual

---

[3] The exception is Prince Hohenlohe, who during his chancellorship (1894–1900) was never foreign minister.

[4] We have likewise erred on the side of inclusion when also including all foreign ministers (many of whom were also federal chancellors) in Austria from 1922 to 1959, although the Austrian Foreign Ministry during this time, for cost-reducing reasons, was formally only an "office" within the Federal Chancellery (Derndarsky 1982: 61, 68).

foreign minister, we have gathered biographical information on 1,155 foreign ministers (some serving multiple terms) from the thirteen selected countries. The data was collected through a team of research assistants knowledgeable in the language of the country they coded, based on web searches and published biographies.

2.2 Background Characteristics of Foreign Ministers

In a classic article, George Modelski (1970) surveyed a global sample of all foreign ministers holding office in 1965. The modal foreign minister in the world at this time was a middle-aged man with university education, no military experience and a background in politics, not diplomacy. As shown in Figure 1, the foreign ministers in our sample of thirteen current and former great powers since 1789 very much align with this general description.

In 1965, only two of the foreign ministers of the world were women (Modelski 1970: 145). In our sample, to this very day (or, more precisely, up until May 2017), only thirty-one women have served as foreign ministers. First among them was Karin Söder, Sweden's foreign minister in 1976–1978, followed by five other Swedish foreign ministers since. Other relatively early examples are Susanna Agnelli, foreign minister of Italy in 1995–1996, and Tansu Ciller of Turkey in 1996–1997. Among the current great powers, only the United Kingdom and the United States have had female foreign ministers, the United Kingdom briefly so (Margaret Becket in 2006–2007), whereas the

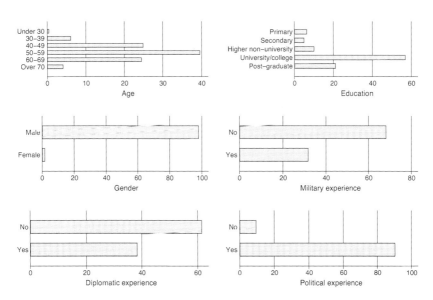

Figure 1 Personal characteristics of foreign ministers (percentages).

United States has had three: Madeleine Albright (1997–2001), Condoleezza Rice (2005–2009), and Hilary Clinton (2009–2013).

When it comes to age, the youngest foreign ministers in our sample are Prince Komatsu Akihito of Japan, who at the age of twenty-two served a short stint as foreign minister at the very beginning of the Meiji restoration in 1868, and Manuel Godoy, who in 1792 at the age of twenty-five became secretary of state for Spain, and remained so for six years. The oldest are Suzuki Kantaro, who at the age of seventy-eight became the prime minister of Japan in April 1945 and for two days simultaneously held the position as foreign minister, and Pietro Nenni, who at the age of seventy-seven served some nine months as foreign minister of Italy in 1968–1969. The foreign ministers in our sample have been fifty-four years on average when entering office, but this average has been on the rise historically. In the early nineteenth century, the typical foreign minister was in his mid-forties, whereas in the twenty-first century, the average age at entering office is fifty-seven years. While there is some change over time in this regard, the fact that foreign ministers are middle-aged has thus changed very little. It is also a characteristic that is very stable across countries.

Having a higher education has always been a hallmark of foreign ministers, but increasingly so over time. Already by the early nineteenth century, more than two-thirds of foreign ministers in our sample had a university degree or higher; since the 1930s, around 90 percent did so. This remarkably stable figure conceals some interesting variation among countries, however. Foreign ministers from China, the Ottoman Empire, and Russia/USSR have generally had lower levels of education. This to some extent also applies to Spain, but in this case largely due to the large number of Spanish foreign ministers appointed in the nineteenth century. But foreign ministers as a cast are more or less everywhere quite far from the everyday man or woman in the street. In our entire sample, only 11 percent had no more than a primary or secondary education. Yet, and perhaps somewhat surprisingly, some of the most long-serving foreign ministers in history comes from this group of lower-educated people. This goes for Count Nesselrode of Russia (1816–1856) and Vyacheslav Molotov (1939–1949) of the Soviet Union, for example, but also, in more recent times, Carl Bildt of Sweden (2006–2014) and Joshka Fisher of Germany (1998–2005).

We now turn to the foreign ministers' background experience in serving other functions, where we distinguish between military, diplomatic, and political experience. While Figure 1 (again) captures the overall characteristics of the whole sample, Figures 2–3 break this variation down over time and space. Again, in line with Modelski (1970), the majority of foreign ministers in our sample, or 68 percent, lack military background, in terms of education, service,

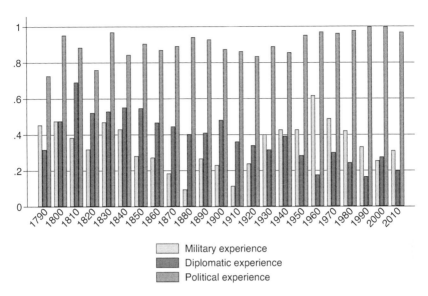

Figure 2 Three types of background experience over time (shares).

or professionally. There is, however, variation across both time and space with respect to that rule.

As seen in Figure 2, reflecting the ebb and flow of major wars in the international system, there were more foreign ministers with military experience both after the Napoleonic wars in the early nineteenth century and after the Second World War in the twentieth. Figure 3, moreover, makes clear that Germany has throughout its history predominantly had a relative preference for putting someone with military experience on the post as foreign minister. This applies, not surprisingly, most conspicuously for Prussia, renowned for being a highly militarized state, having 72 percent of its foreign ministers from the military. But even after the Second World War, 57 percent of Germanys foreign ministers have military experience, although that today typically only means having completed military service, something which also applies to all Turkish foreign ministers (except the single female one). Two other outliers are France and the United States, which have had almost as many foreign ministers with military background as without one. After Prussia/Germany, where half of all foreign ministers even have some combat experience, France is also the country where most foreign ministers have experience from the battlefield (in the French case this applies to 27 percent of the foreign ministers).

Perhaps somewhat surprisingly, foreign ministers overall have predominantly *not* had personal experience with diplomatic service abroad. As shown in Figure 3, this particularly applies to Italy, the United Kingdom, and the United

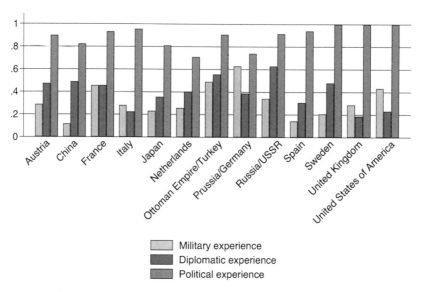

Figure 3 Three types of background experience across countries (shares).

States, where only some 20 percent of the foreign ministers have diplomatic background. Spain and Turkey (since 1922) are also among the countries where this is more unusual, with some 30 percent having diplomatic experience, whereas in Austria, China, France, and Sweden, it is almost as common to have a foreign minister with as without diplomatic experience. Only in Russia, particularly during tsarist time, Prussia, and the Ottoman Empire, was diplomatic experience a modal feature. As these historical examples attest to, Figure 2 shows that a background in diplomacy was much more common in the nineteenth century than it is today. Yet even in cases like the United States, where diplomatic experience is the exception, there are prominent examples of secretaries of state with such experience. For example, Madeline Albright was Ambassador to the United Nations before being appointed to become Secretary of State, and even Thomas Jefferson, the first US Secretary of State in our sample, had diplomatic experience before appointment, having been Minister to France for five years.

In terms of political experience more generally, foreign ministers are clearly no rookies. When counting membership in a political party or background in a legislature, in the cabinet, or other higher government office, only 10 percent of the foreign ministers in our sample *lack* any such experience. A modern-day example that has received some attention is President Donald Trump's 2017 appointment to US Secretary of State of Rex Tillerson, a former energy executive without any political experience other than having been a long-time contributor to the Republican Party. Tillerson sat on this post for only a little over a year, but before him the United States had *never* had a foreign minister lacking any kind of political experience,[5] a feature they – as Figure 3 makes clear – share with Sweden and the United Kingdom. Giulio Terzi di Sant'Agata, Italy's foreign minister in 2011–2013, is another rare exception to the rule that foreign ministers come from politics – but Terzi was at least a trained and very experienced diplomat. Another interesting partial exception historically was the Netherlands, which from around the mid-nineteenth to the mid-twentieth century had a tradition of quite a few foreign ministers without political experience according to our definition, one prominent example being Herman Adriaan van Karnebeck, the fifth longest-serving foreign minister in Dutch history (in office from 1918 to 1927), although he had been the Mayor of the Hague before the appointment. Also in Germany, prior to the Second World War, having a foreign minister without political experience was more common than in other countries. There is an overall trend, as shown in Figure 2, toward foreign ministers becoming more and more political professionals. Since 1950, only seven foreign ministers in our entire sample have lacked political experience.

Among types of political experience, having sat in parliament (64 percent) or being member of a political party (62 percent) is clearly the most prominent examples. Fewer have been cabinet ministers (54 percent) or held a higher government office (44 percent). About a fourth (28 percent) of our foreign ministers have served in that position before. The record terms in office in our sample is held by Mehmed Emin Ali Pasha and Mehmed Esad Safvet Pasha, both serving nine times as foreign ministers of the Ottoman Empire.

2.3 Tenure in Office and Mode of Exit of Foreign Ministers

The mean days of tenure for a foreign minister in our sample is 807 days, or little more than two years, but the median is only 411 days, so there is a long tail of unusually long-tenured foreign ministers. In Table 1 we present the "hall of fame" of the ten most long-termed ones in our sample. The most long-lived minister is Count Karl Nesselrode, who served as foreign minister for the Russian Empire for almost fourty years. Next in line is Clemens von Metternich, already mentioned, serving as the foreign minister (and for a long time also chancellor) of the Austrian Empire in 1809–1848. Third is the Soviet Cold War architect Andrei Gromyko (28 years). Fourth is Otto von Bismarck,

---

[5] Two partial exceptions are John W. Foster (1892–1893) and Bainbridge Colby (1920–1921), but – unlike Tillerson – they had both been active in party politics prior to their appointment to Secretary of State.

Table 1 Foreign minister's "hall of fame"

Name	Country	Date of entry	Date of exit	Days
Karl Nesselrode	Russia/ USSR	1816–8–21	1856–4–15	14482
Clemens von Metternich	Austria	1809–10–8	1848–3–13	14036
Andrey Gromyko	Russia/ USSR	1957–2–15	1985–7–2	10364
Otto von Bismarck	Prussia/ Germany	1862–11–23	1890–3–20	9979
Aleksandr Gorchakov	Russia/ USSR	1856–4–27	1882–4–9	9478
Aixin-Jueluo Yiyin (Prince Gong)	China/Qing Empire	1861–1–20	1884–4–8	8479
Aixin-Jueluo Yikuang (Prince Qing)	China/Qing Empire	1884–4–12	1901–7–24	6311
Östen Undén	Sweden	1945–8–12	1962–9–20	6248
Verstolk van Soelen	Netherlands	1825–12–1	1841–9–13	5765
Lars von Engeström	Sweden	1809–3–15	1824–6–8	5564

who first became foreign minister of Prussia in 1862, then kept this post in the North German Confederation from 1866 and, in combination with the post as chancellor, in the unified German Empire from 1871 to 1890 (28 years). Other long-serving foreign ministers include Alexandr Gorkachov, Nesselrode's successor (26 years); Prince Gong, founder of Zongli Yamen, the first Chinese Ministry of Foreign Affairs (23 years); his successor Prince Qing (17 years); as well as Östen Undén, Social Democratic architect of Swedish foreign policy during the Cold War (also 17 years).

As Figure 4 makes clear, the number of days a foreign minister stays in office varies quite substantially across countries. This, in turn, means that different countries have had a very different number of foreign ministers since inception. Spain, for example, has had no less than 187 foreign ministers between 1789 and 2017, making up for an average time in office of only 429 days. Japan has had 121 foreign ministers since 1868, for an average of 451 days. France is third, with 177 foreign ministers since 1789 and an average tenure in office of only 469 days. The high volatility in office in Spain and France is, however, largely a nineteenth-century phenomenon, a trend that is also visible in other countries: before the First World War, the average number of days in office was

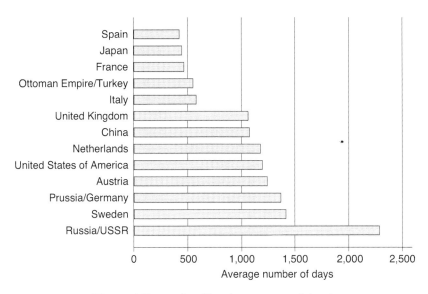

Figure 4 Tenure in office (average no of days).

851 days; after the Second World War, it is 978 days. The country with the longest tenures overall is Russia, where only thirty-five foreign ministers have served since 1789, for an average of 2,292 days (or about 6 years).

Not all foreign ministers leave their posts for the same reason. We have thus also collected information on the primary modes through which they exited office, presented in Table 2. Some 2 percent die by natural causes on their post, such as Nobel Laureate Gustav Stresemann, who suffered from a stroke on October 3, 1929, while still foreign minister of the Weimar Republic. Some 4 percent face a more violent ousting, such as revolution (Max von Baden in Germany in 1918), deposition by a foreign power (Wilhelm Wolf during die Anschluss in Austria in 1938), or even assassination (Walter Rathenau of Germany in 1922, Englebert Dolfuss of Austria in 1934, and Anna Lindh of Sweden in 2003). A more common exit reason is retirement due to ill health or other types of unforced resignations (18 percent), but the most common exit is simply that the term of the entire cabinet reaches its end, primarily due to term limits, elections, or other constitutionally mandated government terminations (40 percent).

In line with our theorizing of the principal-agent relationship between the foreign minister and his or her HoG, presented in Section 1, the mode of exit that mainly concerns us in this Element is what we call *forced resignation*, comprising slightly less than a third of the sample of foreign minister spells (31 percent). This is when the foreign minister is *involuntarily* removed from office by the HoG (who, to repeat, could also be the head of state). The reasons for such removals vary, but

Table 2 Why foreign ministers lose office

Mode of exit	N	Percent
Death by natural cause	22	1.9
Violently	42	3.6
Retirement/unforced resignation	203	17.6
End of government term	457	39.6
Forced resignation	354	30.6
Missing:		
Incumbent	13	1.1
Unknown	64	5.5
TOTAL	1,155	100 %

Note: The "forced resignation" category consists of nine subcategories, with the following primary reasons for removals by the HoG (# of occurrences in parentheses): "Political scandal" (14), "Policy disagreement between minister and premier/PM" (39), "Policy disagreement between minister and monarch/president" (57), "Policy disagreement between minister and own party/other minister" (36), "Personal/departmental error or low personal performance" (24), "Move to other post within cabinet" (69), "Move to another post within cabinet in the general context of a reshuffle" (53), "Loss of eligibility for the post" (3), and "Other reason" (59).

most importantly consist of political or policy disagreements: about 11 percent of the foreign ministers leave their post due to a disagreement with the premier, president, or monarch, or the party leadership. US Secretary of State Colin Powell is a prominent example of an individual leaving office due to a policy disagreement with the president. In a 2004 *Washington Post* article, Powell expressed discontent with the George W. Bush administration's decision to invade Iraq in 2003, and was after that not re-appointed when Bush was re-elected in 2004 (instead of being replaced by Condoleezza Rice).

Another fairly common type of forced resignation is that foreign ministers leave their post in some kind of reshuffle of the cabinet (11 percent of the exits). Either they are the only cabinet member being moved to another post or there is a general reshuffle involving several ministers. In the summer of 1989, for example, UK prime minister Margaret Thatcher suddenly replaced Foreign Secretary Geoffrey Howe after the latter had threatened with resignation over a policy disagreement on British participation in the European Monetary System. Howe was instead appointed deputy prime minister, by most observers considered a demotion. Another example is Robert Schuman, one of the original architects of what was to become the European Union and French minister of foreign affairs in 1948–1953. Schuman was deposed from his post and instead appointed Minister of Justice after a row over French foreign policy toward its Moroccan possession.

Considering that scandals involving cabinet members are given so much attention in the media, the number of foreign ministers leaving office due to a scandal is surprisingly small – only about 1 percent leave their post due to such a reason. Somewhat more common are exits from this post due to personal or departmental error – about 2 percent of the ministers leave their post due to this reason.

The occurrence of forced resignations is fairly evenly distributed across countries, but with some exceptions. It is much less common that Italian ministers for foreign affairs get forced out of office; since unification, this has only happened in 8 percent of the cases (instead, it is much more common than in other countries that ministers of foreign affairs in Italy resign because their governments reach the end of their term). By contrast, it is much more common in Spain and Germany, with around 50 percent of all foreign ministers being deposed in this manner. But in both these cases, the high occurrence is largely a historical phenomenon. In Spain, the bulk of forced resignations occurred during the turbulent nineteenth century, during the restoration and the second republic in the 1930s. A similar story goes for Germany, where the bulk of these resignations happened in Prussia, prior to unification, and then in Imperial, Weimar, and Nazi Germany. After the Second World War, only 17 percent of Spanish, and 7 percent of German foreign ministers have been forced out of office involuntarily. As these country trajectories suggest, forced resignations have become somewhat less common over time. Before the First World War, about 37 percent of the foreign ministers in our sample left office through forced resignation. After the Second World War, this occurrence has dropped to around 20 percent.

2.4 Conclusion

Based on a sample of thirteen current and former great powers since 1789, this section has drawn a portrait of the typical foreign minister. Foreign ministers are, to this day, almost always men. They tend to be highly educated and in their fifties when entering office. In their previous careers, they have not served in the military, nor in the diplomatic corps. This is in line with the work of Modelski (1970), who shows that most foreign ministers have a university education and rarely have military experience. Instead, they are men of politics, most often legislative and party politics.

The foreign ministers remain in office for a few years, and when they leave, it is most of the time because of constitutionally mandated terminations of the governments for which they serve. Almost a third, however, are forced out of office by their head of government, mostly due to policy disagreements or in ministerial reshuffles. Such forced resignations may suggest, in line with the theoretical framework we presented in the first section of this Element, that heads of government as principals use their ability to fire foreign ministers when they do not act in line with the wishes of the HoG.

So, what explains these patterns? Why do some personal characteristics recur so prominently among foreign ministers? And what are the consequences of these characteristics, as well as the political contexts under which foreign ministers serve, for how long they remain in office? These are the questions to which we now turn.

3 What Explains Who Is Appointed as Foreign Minister?

We have in the previous section shown that, in the thirteen current and former great powers we analyze in this Element, foreign ministers tend to have been men of politics, having had a career within the party or in legislative politics before appointment. We also show that their previous careers have typically not been within the military or diplomatic corps. However, there is some variation over time and across countries in the type of background that the foreign ministers have. This section of the Element focuses on this variation and asks who is appointed as foreign minister in a certain context, and whether it matters who the leader making the appointment is.

We here draw on the comparative literature on ministerial selection that we described in Section 1, which departs from a view of political systems as based upon a chain of delegation in which the HoG acts as "principal" of the ministers who are acting as "agents." As described in Section 1, the principal can employ several control mechanisms to mitigate agency loss, that is, to avoid that the ministers as agents act against the wishes of the principal. A main way to avoid agency loss is to apply *ex ante* control mechanisms such as extensive screening of potential candidates for ministerial posts (e.g. Strøm 2003). Hence, careful selection among potential candidates is highly important.

Drawing on the principal-agent framework described in Section 1, we hypothesize that politicians with similar backgrounds to their HoGs (or state) are more likely to become foreign ministers, since HoGs expect that such ministers will have similar preferences to their own. For example, we ask, is a HoG who has a military background more likely to want to surround himself or herself with advisors who have a background within the military. We also hypothesize that politicians who are experienced foreign policy makers, diplomats, or have a military background will be appointed when the country faces a geopolitical environment characterized by uncertainty, since such foreign ministers are likely to be expected to perform well under such circumstances, which should be valued by a HoG.

To evaluate these hypotheses, we merge our historical data on the background of foreign ministers in thirteen current or former great powers over 200 years with data on HoG attributes and on contextual features, such as the level of conflict that a country faces at a certain point in time. Before turning to describing the data used in this section, we turn to describing the specific hypotheses to be evaluated about the appointment of foreign ministers.

3.1 Expectations about the Appointment of Foreign Ministers

We are interested in the personnel decisions made by HoGs, during times of peace as well as before and after conflicts, and we should thus take our starting point in the interests and goals that these leaders have. Following the previous literature on war and leadership survival, and the comparative literature on ministers, HoGs (prime ministers, president, kings, or dictators) are assumed to be interested in staying in office; that is, they are assumed to be office-seeking (see, e.g., Bueno de Mesquita and Siverson 1995; Bueno de Mesquita et al. 2003; Kam and Indridason 2005). In democratic systems this implies that they are instrumentally vote-seeking; that is, they should to some extent aim to "please their voters" in order to stay in office (e.g., Dewan and Dowding 2005). In addition, leaders in any regime may also be policy-seeking in the sense that they are interested in implementing a specific policy program. For office-, policy-, or vote-seeking reasons, leaders should be interested in hiring individual ministers who are likely to perform well, and who are likely to be loyal and act in the interests of the principal, and in making personnel decisions that minimize agency loss.

We here focus on the backgrounds of foreign ministers, since such features may influence foreign policy making (Saunders 2017). We highlight three possible relationships between leader experience and foreign minister experience: affinity, complementarity, and performance. The affinity argument focuses on the idea that leaders prefer foreign ministers who are like them. The complementarity argument focuses on the idea that leaders will aim to appoint foreign ministers who complement them in terms of skills. Performance arguments focus on the idea that some characteristics of the foreign ministers lead to "better" foreign policy making, which may be especially important during specific times, such as when the country faces a foreign policy threat.

As mentioned earlier, a main argument in the comparative literature on ministerial selection is that HoGs, as principals, should aim to appoint ministers, as agents, who are less likely to engage in "ministerial drift" when given the power over a department (see e.g. Kam et al. 2010). One way for the HoG to do so is to appoint ministers with similar views as they have themselves. As we are here focusing on background features of ministers, we specify this "affinity" hypothesis somewhat differently, but drawing on the same idea, and hypothesize that:

H1: HoGs are likely to appoint foreign ministers with backgrounds similar to their own.

The underlying assumption is that individual politicians' backgrounds also signal something about their preferences and views, which is an assumption that has been made in the previous comparative literature on ministerial selection (e.g., Alexiadou 2016).

Our second hypothesis draws on the idea that "complementarity" between leaders and advisors matter (Saunders 2017). We argue, drawing on previous work, that an inexperienced HoG is simply more in need and can more credibly delegate power to experienced foreign policy advisors, and we thus hypothesize that:

H2: (in)experienced HoGs are (more) less likely to appoint experienced foreign ministers.

To clarify, there may be several reasons for why an inexperienced leader "needs" an experienced foreign minister. First, for policy-making reasons, a less experienced leader may need an experienced advisor to help him or her make competent foreign policy decisions. Second, for vote-seeking reasons, an inexperienced leader may feel the need to show the electorate that the country's foreign policy is handled in a competent manner, which can be done by delegating power to a foreign minister with a high (perceived) level of competence. An experienced leader is not likely to have such a "need" to appoint experienced advisors, and may avoid doing so, and appoint an inexperienced foreign minister, to keep foreign policy power for him or herself.

Drawing on the literature on leadership survival and war (e.g., Chiozza and Goemans 2011; Croco and Weeks 2016), we also expect that contextual features, related to international conflicts, matter for foreign minister selection, and could influence which background a politician should have to be appointed. We here suggest that certain individuals may be expected to perform well in conflictual or threatening situations. We follow the previous literature that suggests that politicians with foreign policy expertise are better able to handle foreign policy decision-making. The argument is that foreign policy "experts" should be able to, for example, assess which information is important, and use their skills or previous experience to make "correct," quick and efficient decisions (Saunders 2017: 224). These abilities should be especially important when the country is exposed to a foreign policy threat. We thus hypothesize that:

H3: HoGs facing a foreign policy threat are more likely to appoint foreign ministers with foreign policy expertise.

As mentioned, the literature on foreign minister survival has stressed that it matters whether a leader operates in a democratic or nondemocratic setting. As argued by Quiroz Flores (2009), whether foreign ministers are seen as a potential challenger to the leader should matter for ministerial selection. Quiroz Flores and Smith (2011) suggest that since threats such as coups are more salient in autocracies, autocrats should feel more threatened by high-performing cabinet ministers, as they are potential challengers to the leader. We draw on this literature here, and hypothesize that:

H4: HoGs in nondemocratic regimes are less likely to appoint politically experienced foreign ministers.

3.2 HoG Attributes, Contextual features, and Foreign Minister Experience

To create our dependent and independent variables used in this section's analyses, we have merged our dataset on foreign minister backgrounds with other historical datasets, allowing us to examine how the context and leader background influence which individuals become foreign ministers. To do so, we have here merged our data with the *Leader Experience and Attribute Descriptions* dataset (*LEAD*), which includes information on leaders' backgrounds (from 1875), for example, describing their upbringing and military experience (Horowitz et al. 2015), and with the *Militarized Interstate Disputes* (MID) dataset (Palmer et al. 2015) in order to capture contextual factors such as ongoing conflict.

To specify the dependent variable when evaluating the hypothesis that leaders will appoint foreign ministers with backgrounds similar to their own (H1), we need similar information on the backgrounds of leaders and foreign ministers. Since our coding scheme was inspired by the LEAD coding scheme, we can straightforwardly create such a variable. We here focus on the military background of leaders and foreign ministers. An important reason for doing so is that the military background of politicians is likely to influence or say something about their foreign policy preferences and behavior. For example, several scholars have shown that the military experience of leaders influence their likelihood of initiating and escalating disputes (Chiozza and Choi 2003; Horowitz and Stam 2014). We thus include a dependent variable describing if the foreign minister has a *Military background*. The independent variables used to measure HoGs' military background is drawn from the LEAD dataset, and describes if the leader had a *Military career* before appointment and if the leader has *Combat experience*, with the latter variable signaling that the leader had clearly been active within the military.

To create our dependent variable aimed at evaluating the idea that (in) experienced leaders are (more) less likely to appoint experienced foreign ministers (H2), we specify a variable which describes if the foreign minister or secretary of state has previously served in this office, measuring the *Foreign minister experience* of the (re-)appointed minister. To specify the independent variable to evaluate this hypothesis, we again make use of the LEAD dataset, which includes information on *Leader tenure* (in years), which should signal how much experience the leader has in handling foreign policy decisions.

Our third hypothesis suggests that leaders operating in a threatening or conflictual situation are more likely to appoint foreign ministers with foreign policy expertise (H3). To evaluate this hypothesis, we need to elaborate on what "foreign policy expertise" is and how it can be measured. Here, we first suggest that the diplomatic experience of foreign ministers should be important to consider since these ministers have a specific role within the cabinet, leading negotiations with other countries' representatives (see, e.g., Quiroz Flores 2009: 118). Having diplomatic experience should thus increase a politician's ability to handle international negotiations, and could thus be more important during wartime or when the country is exposed to foreign policy threat, because they are expected to perform well in this position. We therefore perform analyses where the dependent variable describes if the foreign minister had *Diplomatic experience* or not.

However, we also expect that previous experience as a foreign minister will increase the foreign policy expertise of a politician, and we thus also analyze this dependent variable (specified above) when evaluating this hypothesis. Lastly, we also analyze the military experience of the foreign minister to evaluate this hypothesis, as military expertise could be perceived as being a useful type of foreign policy expertise when the country is at war or faces a foreign policy threat. Hence, to evaluate hypothesis three, we look at three background features, focusing on foreign ministers' diplomatic and military experience, and their previous foreign ministers experience.

We use two basic independent variables to evaluate H3, which gauge whether the country faces a foreign policy threat, focusing on a variable from the MID dataset (Palmer et al. 2015), which specifies if the country is (when the foreign minister is appointed) involved in an international *Conflict*, and three dichotomous variables that specifies whether the appointment of the foreign minister occurred during major great power conflicts, namely the *First World War* (1914–1918), the *Second World War* (1939–1945), or during the *Cold War period* (1957–1991).[6]

Drawing on the work by Quiroz Flores and Smith (2011), our last hypothesis says that leaders in autocratic regimes are less likely to appoint politically experienced foreign ministers (H4), since these individuals may be perceived as challengers, and whose appointment increases the risk that the leader loses his or her power. Here, we focus on whether a foreign minister has a political background before appointment. The main independent variable that we analyze here is a variable describing the extent to which a country was a *Democracy* or autocracy at the time that the foreign minister was appointed, drawing on the *V-Dem* polyarchy measure (Teorell et al. 2019). To account for potentially varying effects of wars in autocracies and democracies (Chiozza and Goemans 2011; Croco and Weeks 2016), we also interact the conflict variable with the level of democracy. This interaction effectively captures the effect of conflict on different political institutions.

We also include several control variables that may influence the selection of ministers, mainly drawing on the variables included in the LEAD dataset and in our data on foreign ministers. We refer to these variables as controls rather than confounders, as our research design does not focus on causal relationships and rather highlights plausible connections and correlations. Yet, by including these controls, we can estimate the partial effect of our key independent variables to test our hypotheses. First, we control for the leader's *Age* (and *Age squared*), their gender (*Female leader*), and their *Education*. The quadratic polynomial for age is a standard functional form that captures the importance of an individual's middle age. In other words, it allows us to gauge whether the relationship with age is curvilinear. Second, we control for several country-level features, describing if the country is currently a *Great power*, how many *Great powers* there are in the

---

[6] We have also performed analyses using other, more complex measures of "foreign policy threat," for example including a variable measuring the geopolitical threat that a country is exposed to at a specific point in time drawing on Markowitz and Fariss (2018: 78). Results using such a variable are similar to the ones presented here. Also note that we cannot include the French revolutionary wars or the Napoleonic wars among the major great power conflicts, since they occurred before the LEAD data start in the mid-nineteenth century.

international system, and how many countries that border to the country (*Total borders*).

Finally, since the different types of background experience of foreign ministers to some extent overlap, for each type of analysis with one experience as the dependent variables we control for the other experiences. It should be kept in mind, however, that since we do not know the pool of candidates from which a foreign minister was drawn when appointed, our results should be considered correlational.

3.3 Patterns of Foreign Minister Selection

In Section 2 we described the patterns of foreign minister backgrounds in all the countries over the study period, focusing on the shares of foreign ministers with various backgrounds across decades. Here we saw some interesting patterns. First, looking at political experience of foreign ministers, we saw that this has been important during the entire period, but that there is a slight increasing trend over time, suggesting that foreign ministers are increasingly being picked among the political rank. Looking at the diplomatic experience, we find the opposite trend – diplomatic experience among the foreign ministers has become less important over time. When it comes to military experience, we do not see any such trends, but instead there seems to be a fluctuating pattern with more foreign ministers with military experience both after the Napoleonic wars in the early nineteenth century and after the Second World War in the twentieth. This may suggest that foreign ministers with a military background are more important to appoint when the country faces some specific situation, for example, when facing the risk of war.

We now turn to studying the role of various leadership and contextual features in foreign minister appointment using multivariate models, which allows us to control for various features when analyzing the impact of a specific feature. Since we are dealing with dichotomous dependent variables, we here rely on probit models to estimate the effect of variables on the likelihood of a foreign minister having a particular background. We present coefficient plots (marginal effects) with 95 percent confidence intervals. Positive coefficients indicate an increase in the probability that a foreign minister has a particular characteristic, while negative coefficients indicate a decrease in this probability. In all models, we cluster the standard errors by country.

In Figure 5, we present the model aimed at evaluating H1, which says that leaders with military background should appoint foreign ministers with a similar *military experience*. Here we first see that foreign ministers with military background are less likely to also have diplomatic background, but once we control for

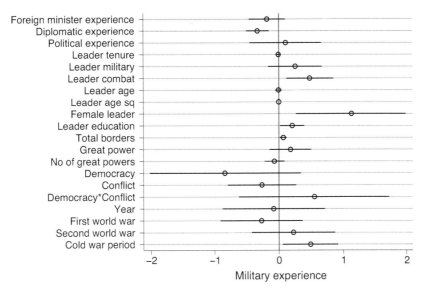

Figure 5 Marginal effects of various features on military experience (95% CIs).

Note: Results from probit models using our FM dataset merged with the LEAD dataset, covering FM appointments during the time period 1856–2004 in thirteen countries ($N = 652$). Standard errors clustered on country.

other background experiences, the effect of the variable measuring the *leader's combat* experience is positive and significant, whereas the coefficient for the more basic military career variable is not. Hence, the results suggest that leaders with considerable military experience are more likely to appoint foreign ministers with military experience. If our assumption is correct that individuals with a (clear) military background share similar foreign policy preferences, this suggests that leaders choose advisors who they expect will implement policies that they themselves prefer. Hence, specific individuals are appointed to limit agency loss when power over foreign policy is delegated.

An example of a famous Secretary of State who had military experience is Henry Kissinger, who served first under President Richard Nixon in the 1970s. Kissinger was in combat during the Second World War when the United States made advancements into Germany. He was a Counter Intelligence Corps Special Agent and Sergeant, also being awarded the Bronze Star – hence, clearly having extensive military experience. Nixon also had military experience, having served in the US Navy during the Second World War, reaching the position as Commander. Biographical work also suggest that Kissinger and Nixon shared many beliefs regarding foreign policy, both seeing themselves as foreign policy realists (see, e.g., Dallek 2007).

We now turn to evaluating H3, which says that we should see more foreign ministers with a military experience, as a form of foreign policy expertise, when the country is at war, or when the situation is particularly insecure or threatening. An example of a foreign minister with extensive military experience serving when the country was facing a war is Colin Powell, who became Secretary of State in 2001, appointed by President George W. Bush. Powell was a professional soldier for thirty-five years, and he held a number of positions within the military, rising to the rank of general, and taking part in combat during the Vietnam war. Powell was US Secretary of State during the September 11th (2001) terror attack; he was a key figure in the US-led coalition in the War on Terrorism, and he was Secretary of State during the 2003 US invasion of Iraq. Our statistical results with respect to this particular feature are, however, mixed. We find that the coefficient for the *Cold War* variable is positive and significant, supporting the idea that individuals with military background are more likely to be appointed as foreign ministers when the country faces a foreign policy threat. Yet, the world war variables are not significant, nor is the effect of a country being involved in an actual conflict (whether in democracies or autocracies), as indicated by the null effect of the variables *Conflict* and its interaction with the level of *Democracy*.

We do not present a lengthy discussion of the effects of our control variables. Yet, we note some interesting results for the gender variable – our results suggest that female HoGs are more likely to appoint foreign ministers with a military experience. Here it should be noted that our sample includes few female HoGs, and that the results could be driven by some particular cases. In fact, only two female leaders, Margareth Thatcher, who was UK's prime minister between 1979 and 1990, and Tancu Ciller, who was the prime minister of Turkey between 1993 and 1996, are included in our analysis, accounting for the appointment of ten foreign ministers.

In Figure 6, we shift our focus to looking at previous experience of being foreign minister as dependent variable. We start by evaluating H2, which suggests that inexperienced leaders will appoint advisors who have a lot of foreign policy experience. The effect of the variable measuring the leader's tenure in office is negative and significant, suggesting that the hypothesis is supported – the fewer years the leader has been in office, the more likely they are to appoint foreign ministers who have previously headed the foreign ministry. One reason for doing so is that a less experienced leader may need an experienced advisor to help him or her make competent foreign policy decisions. To mention an example here, the diplomat Karl von Nesselrode became Russian foreign minister in 1816, and stayed in this post for forty years, thereby being the longest-serving foreign minister in our dataset, and serving under several

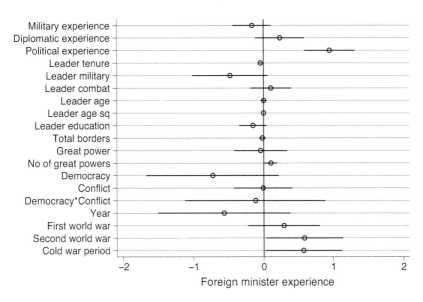

Figure 6 Effects of various features on previous FM experience (95% CIs).

Note: Results from probit models using our FM dataset merged with the LEAD dataset, covering FM appointments during the time period 1856–2004 in thirteen countries ($N = 642$). Gender (Female leader) is dropped here due to a lack of variation. Standard errors clustered on country.

emperors, some who were clearly very inexperienced. Nesselrode was part of leading the so-called Holy Alliance, a coalition between the great powers of Austria, Prussia, and Russia, and he was a key contributor to the peace system established after the Napoleonic wars.

If we instead look at the independent variables measuring whether the foreign minister was appointed during a conflict, both the *Second World War* and the *Cold War period* coefficient are positive and significant. We thus find support in this case for the expectation (H3) that we should see an increase in the foreign minister with previous experience in the office. Yet, again, we do not find similar results for the *Conflict* variable – the impact of this variable is nonexistent (both in autocracies and democracies).

Turning to our third dependent variable in Figure 7, focusing on whether a foreign minister has a *diplomatic experience*, we do not find many significant effects – hence, we are not really able to explain the variation in this variable. We hypothesized that foreign ministers with a diplomatic background would be appointed when the country faces war or foreign policy threat, but neither the *Conflict* variable nor the specific war variables exerts a significant effect here. Hence, H3 is not given any support looking at diplomatic background as

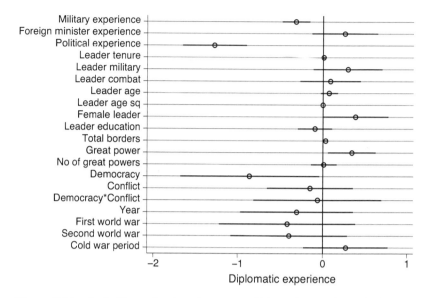

Figure 7 Marginal effects of various features on diplomatic experience (95% CIs).

Note: Results from probit models using our FM dataset merged with the LEAD dataset, covering FM appointments during the time period 1856–2004 in thirteen countries ($N = 652$). Standard errors clustered on country.

"expertise." With both military and political expertise variables exerting a negative and significant influence here, we also see that the foreign ministers with a diplomatic background are a rather unique set of actors. Only the democracy variable exerts a significant effect in this analysis, showing that diplomatic experience is less common among foreign ministers appointed in democratic contexts.

Lastly, in Figure 8, we analyze what features are correlated with the *political experience* of foreign ministers. Recall that a political background is very common among foreign ministers, and that few foreign ministers in our sample (about 10%) do not have such a background. For this reason, we cannot control for other background experiences in the statistical model but instead construct a slightly different dependent variable that is coded as zero if a foreign minister has either diplomatic or military background. In this setup, our results are in line with H4 that leaders in autocracies are more likely to appoint foreign ministers without political experience (the effect of the democracy variable is positive and significant also if not interacted with *conflict*). We expect the mechanism underlying this effect is that autocratic leaders see individuals with a political career as potential challengers to their own office. Interestingly, however, the effect is the opposite when a country is

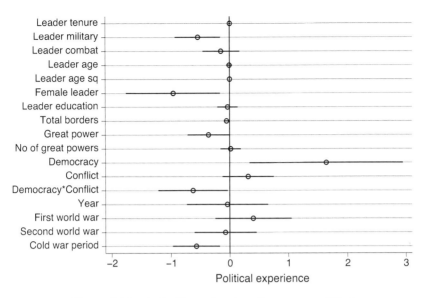

Figure 8 Marginal effects of various features on political
experience only (95% CIs).

Note: Results from probit models using our FM dataset merged with the LEAD dataset, covering FM appointments during the time period 1856–2004 in thirteen countries ($N = 653$). Standard errors clustered on country.

experiencing *Conflict*, meaning that then it is instead autocratic leaders who are more likely to appoint politically experienced foreign ministers. This is an intriguing result worthy of further study,

Somewhat surprisingly, the leader's military background seems to be negatively correlated with foreign ministers' political background. Our results thus suggest that a leader who has had a military background is less likely to appoint a foreign minister with a political background. This may suggest that there is a sort of trade-off between politicians who have a political background and who have a military background, and that leaders with a military background are more interested in appointing foreign ministers with a similar background to their own. Another result our theory cannot account for is that foreign ministers with *only* a political background were less likely to be appointed during the *Cold War* period.

3.4 Conclusion

The aim of this section has been to answer the question of why some individuals become foreign ministers, motivated by the fact that these key actors can significantly influence a country's foreign policy due to their policy expertise, departmental discretion, and since they are the government's primary voice on foreign affairs. We have answered this question by analyzing our dataset that covers foreign minister appointments in thirteen countries since the mid-nineteenth century.

All in all, the results support some of our hypotheses drawing on the theoretical framework presented in section one. Foreign ministers seem to be more likely to have military experience when the leader also has such a background, supporting an "affinity" argument, and the idea that leaders select ministers likely to share their preferences to minimize agency loss. This result is in line with the theoretical argument drawn from authors such as Kam, Bianco, Sened, and Smyth (2010), and Bäck, Debus, and Müller (2016), who suggest that HoGs, as principals, will select those individuals for cabinet whose policy preferences are as close as possible to the principal's own preferences to ensure that the line ministers, as agents, act in accordance with his or her wishes.

We also find that foreign ministers are likely to be more experienced when the leader lacks foreign policy-making experience, which supports a "complementarity" argument. This suggests that leaders select experienced foreign ministers when they are "in need" of politicians likely to perform well in office. This is in line with Saunders' (2017) argument that inexperienced leaders are better able to credibly delegate to experienced secretaries.

We also find some support for the idea that some contextual features matter for foreign minister selection. For example, we find that foreign ministers were more likely to have a military background during the *Cold War* period, and to have previous experience as foreign minister during the Second World War and Cold War period, suggesting that policy expertise is important during times of uncertainty. We also find that foreign ministers with political experience are less common in autocracies, which could suggest that individuals with such experience are perceived as potential challengers by autocratic leaders, who avoid promoting those who might "dethrone" them. This result is in line with the theoretical argument made by Quiroz Flores and Smith (2011), who argue that internal threats such as coups are more salient in autocracies and therefore autocrats do not appoint high performing cabinet ministers, as they are potential challengers to the leader.

4 Why Are Foreign Ministers Fired?

This section explains why some foreign ministers have longer tenure in office than others. In our database of ministerial tenure, foreign ministers stay in office for a median of eight years. However, 25 percent of ministers have a tenure of less than three years, with another 25 percent having a tenure in office of more than seventeen years. What explains this variation in the time in office of these top diplomats and advisors?

Traditionally, work on ministerial tenure has focused on principal-agent theories of cabinet change. According to this view, HoGs use compatible incentives and participation constraints to select and incentivize ministers to successfully complete delegation tasks. In practice, leaders rely on the power to dismiss a minister as an incentive to secure successful delegation (e.g., Strøm 2003) or as an instrument to deal with scandals (e.g., Dewan and Dowding 2005).

More recently, the emphasis has switched to considerations of political survival (Quiroz Flores 2009). In this view, leaders rely on competent cabinet ministers to deliver good policy. However, ministers are also political challengers, and therefore leaders have incentives to keep incompetent individuals in office (Quiroz Flores 2016; Quiroz Flores and Smith 2011). Whether leaders keep competent or mediocre individuals in the cabinet, in turn, depends on political institutions. The argument of political survival as originally developed by Bueno de Mesquita et al. (2003) focuses on the provision of public and private goods to members of their winning coalition. All else equal, in large coalitions, leaders provide more public goods, while in small coalitions, leaders provide more private goods.

The same logic should apply to the goods provided by a Minister of Foreign Affairs, as an agent of the leader. However, it is not straightforward to measure goods provision in international affairs. To fill this gap, Quiroz Flores (2016) proposed a measure of competence for foreign ministers – the avoidance of military disputes by diplomatic means. War is driven by politics, and foreign ministers as countries' top diplomats and advisors are in an ideal position to find negotiated settlements (Fearon 1995). Previously we have made references to Henry Kissinger, US Secretary of State between 1973 and 1977, who is perhaps one of the best examples of a minister with significant influence over the course of multiple international conflicts – he did win a Nobel Peace Prize for the Paris Peace Accords that contributed to the withdrawal of American forces in Vietnam, although the accords were not successful in ending the conflict. Evidently, not all disputes can be avoided, so it is expected that countries, and particularly democratic countries, would fight wars that they are likely to win. In autocratic countries, however, defeat in war may not determine the tenure of a foreign minister or their leader, as survival depends on the provision of private goods. Quiroz Flores (2016) tested this theory using data on international conflict.

In previous work (Bäck et al. 2021), we have tested the hypotheses we present in the following, and found evidence in their favor. This Element improves on that analysis in two ways. First, we use an updated database of foreign ministers that includes the tenure of additional ministers. Second, we use multiple-record data for ministerial tenure and key covariates, including the changing nature of conflict over time. This vastly improves our previous analysis while correcting for technical challenges.

We acknowledge that there is an endogeneity process at work, as ministers should only engage in conflict when it does not affect tenure. Addressing this challenge is beyond the scope of this Element, but we refer readers to the work of Quiroz Flores (2016) for a solution to this endogeneity problem, as well as technical solutions to jointly model ministerial and leader tenure.

4.1 Expectations about the Tenure of Foreign Ministers

Building on previous work analyzing the effect of competence on the tenure of foreign ministers, we argue here that a full test of the effect of competence requires information about the background of ministers. For instance, and all else equal, a minister with diplomatic experience is more likely to find a diplomatic solution to a dispute than a minister without this type of experience. Also, and again all else equal, a minister with military experience would be able to better assess whether victory is more likely than defeat, and therefore they must be more qualified to advice on which wars to fight. In this view, diplomatic and military experience should be associated with ministerial competence and lower risks of deposition, particularly in democratic settings.

In this light, information about ministers' education and experience is crucial to understand their performance and therefore their tenure in office. This Element tests the following hypotheses developed by Bäck et al. (2021):

H1: All else equal, foreign ministers with a diplomatic background have a lower probability of deposition than ministers without this type of background.

H2: All else equal, foreign ministers with a military background have a lower probability of deposition than ministers without this type of background.

Given the emphasis on performance and survival, this section focuses on the interaction between diplomatic and military experience, and the occurrence and outcome of military disputes. Specifically, we are interested in the occurrence of disputes and their outcome. As mentioned, Quiroz Flores (2016) argues that competent ministers should be able to find a negotiated settlement, and therefore it is expected that the occurrence of disputes should increase the probability of dismissal from the cabinet, as this indicates lack of ability to find a negotiated settlement. However, conditional on the occurrence of a dispute, we expect that positive outcomes emerging from the conflict will decrease a minister's likelihood of deposition.

Nevertheless, once a dispute has started, the probability of staying in office may stay constant, and the key determinant of tenure will be the outcome of the dispute. In this light, we propose two additional hypotheses concerning ministerial tenure.

H3: All else equal, the initiation of a dispute increases the probability of deposition of a foreign minister.

H4: All else equal, victory decreases the probability of deposition of a foreign minister, while defeat increases it.

4.2 An Analysis of the Tenure of Foreign Ministers

This section uses survival analysis to understand variation in the tenure of foreign ministers. Survival analysis is widely used in social sciences, and it focuses on the study of time to an event (e.g., Box-Steffensmeier and Jones 2004; Quiroz Flores 2022). The survival analysis in this section is based on multiple-record data where the unit of analysis is the minister-year. In other words, there are multiple lines of data per foreign minister. The sample includes 1,155 ministers (and 3,726 observations).

As described in Section 2, our database records five different types of ministerial resignations and depositions: death by natural causes, retirement and unforced resignation, violent deposition, end of government, and forced resignation. This section focuses on forced resignations, with all other types of resignations and depositions considered as cases that did not experience the relevant event of interest. Of the 1,155 ministers in our sample, 354 ministers were forced to resign. Median survival time is eight years with a standard error of 0.62 years. Minimum duration is one year, while maximum duration is forty-one years. The data covers fifteen countries from 1777 to 2017.

As a first glance of the survival of foreign ministers, Figure 9 presents the Kaplan-Meier estimate of the survival function. The figure is an estimate of the proportion of ministers who are still in office over time. At the beginning, all ministers are in office. Over time, ministers are fired, which means that the proportion of ministers in office decreases. For instance, by year eight, only 50 percent of ministers are still holding office. By year 10, about 40 percent of ministers remain in office.

This figure does not account for the effect of variables on ministers' likelihood of deposition. The latter is often captured by a term called the hazard rate, which in this case is the rate at which ministers are deposed from office from over time.

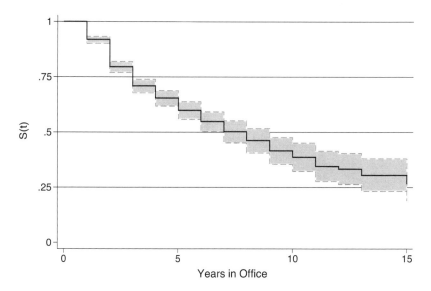

Figure 9 Survival function: Kaplan-Meier estimate.

To explore the effect of variables on this rate of forced resignations, the section uses Cox proportional hazard models. The logic of Cox models is similar to the logic of a linear regression model in that they estimate the effects of independent variables on a dependent variable, which in this case is time to a forced resignation. Specifically, the dependent variable is the number of years in office. All models presented here explore the same independent variables, such as personal characteristics of ministers: diplomatic and military experience. The variables also include controls such as situational aspects related to international disputes and level of democracy.[7] Again, we focus on plausible connections and correlations between the dependent and the independent variables, and we focus our discussion of results on variables directly connected to our hypotheses.

Personal characteristics of ministers are reflected by dummy variables that indicate whether a minister has had a previous term in office (*Previous Term* = 1), whether they had political experience (*Political Experience* = 1), diplomatic experience (*Diplomatic Experience* = 1), military experience (*Military Experience* = 1), whether they are female (*Gender* = 1), and whether they are heads of government (*Head of Government* = 1). Additionally, we consider the age when ministers take office. The variable *Age* has a median of fifty-three years, a maximum of seventy-eight years and a minimum of twenty-two years. We also control for a minister's

---

[7] Our previous work (Bäck et al. 2021) shows that breaking down the analyses by time period (e.g., pre- and post-First World War) does not change the substantive results.

education. The variable *Education* has five possible values: primary, secondary, higher nonuniversity education, university education, and postgraduate education. These categories take values one to five respectively. The median of *Education* is four.

In order to estimate the effect of ministerial performance on tenure, we analyze the role of international disputes. Specifically, we use data on MIDs to account for their occurrence and their outcome (Palmer et al. 2015). The variable *Any Dispute* is a dummy variable equal to one if an MID is active on a particular year. The mean of *Any Dispute* is 0.41, which indicates that 41 percent of observations in the sample present a MID. The variance of this variable is 0.24.

The variables *Number Dispute Win* and *Number Dispute Lose* count the number of victories and defeats in the country's disputes. For the entire sample, the variable *Number Dispute Win* has a mean of 0.05, a minimum of zero, and a maximum of four. Likewise, the variable *Number Dispute Lose* has a mean of 0.01, a minimum of zero, and a maximum of three. For periods of disputes, the means of *Number Dispute Win* and *Number Dispute Lose* are 0.12 and 0.04 respectively, with respective variances 0.13 and 0.04.

In addition, we control for the level of hostility of a dispute. The variable *Mean Dispute Level* is the mean of the maximum level of hostility in active disputes for a particular year. Mean dispute level takes values from zero to five, where zero indicates "No use of force" and five indicates "War." For the entire sample, which includes times without disputes, the mean of this variable is 0.97, with variance of 2.65. For periods with disputes, the mean of this variable is 2.33, with variance of 3.19.

Lastly, the variables *Number Start Any MID* and *Number End Any MID* measure the number of disputes that have started and ended in that year for a particular country. *Number Start Any MID* has a mean of 0.54, minimum of zero, and maximum of 14. The variable *Number End Any MID* has a mean of 0.53, minimum of zero, and maximum of 17. For periods of disputes, the mean of both *Number Start Any MID* and *Number End Any MID* is 1.3, with respective variances 2.24 and 2.34.

Our estimation strategy is as follows. First, we estimate a model that explores the effect of personal characteristics of ministers and domestic political institutions in the absence of international disputes. Technically, this model is the same as all other models, but it restricts the sample to cases where the variable *Any Dispute* is equal to zero. This provides a baseline model that can be compared to models that control for the effect of international conflict. Coefficient plots from this model are presented in Figure 10. Results from a more general model that uses the full sample of observations are presented in Figure 11. For robustness,

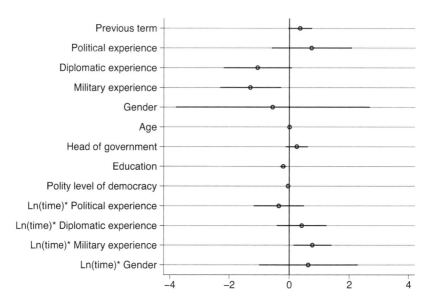

Figure 10 Cox proportional hazards Model 1 (No conflict).

we estimate a third model in Figure 12 that restricts the sample to cases of conflict where the variable *Any Dispute* is equal to one.

All models estimate the Cox model mentioned before.[8] This type of model assumes that the independent variables have the same effect on the dependent variable over time. When this assumption is broken, researchers must identify the cause of the problem (e.g., Keele 2010), correct it (e.g., Licht 2011), and interpret results adequately (e.g., Gandrud 2015; Jones and Metzger 2019). We follow the most up-to-date guidelines to address these challenges (Park and Henry 2015), including the use of interactions between nonproportional covariates and the natural logarithm of tenure.[9] The effect of corrected covariates is complex, and therefore we present conditional linear coefficients to discuss their impact on tenure.

Figures 10 to 12 present coefficient plots along with their 95 percent confidence intervals. Negative coefficients reduce the hazard rate of ministers (consequently increasing their tenure) and positive coefficients increase their hazard rate (thus reducing tenure). Full estimation results are presented in the Appendix.

---

[8] Since there are multiple ministers for the same country, we cluster the standard errors at the country level. Standard errors clustered at the minister level produce similar substantive results. The models use the Efron method for ties, which is particularly useful if we suspect there may be a significant number of tied exits.

[9] Results for the tests of nonproportionality are available in our replication code.

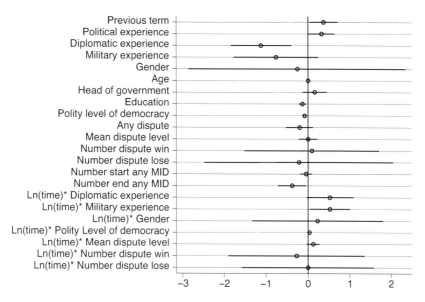

Figure 11 Cox proportional hazards Model 2 (Full sample).

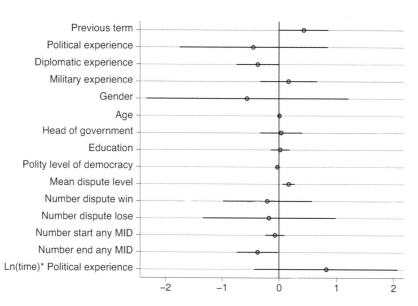

Figure 12 Cox proportional hazards Model 3 (Conflict).

The results for the Models 1 and 2 offer important insights that reveal the effect of ministers' personal characteristics and the occurrence of international conflict. First, while the samples for estimation are very different, many point estimates across models are very similar in their magnitude, direction, and statistical significance. This suggests that the occurrence of international conflict may not have a strong effect on the probability of ministerial deposition.

Variables that capture the personal characteristics of ministers have noticeable effects, although these effects are strongly mediated by the corrections to variables that break the proportionality assumption. Consider the effect of *Diplomatic Experience*. In H1 we argued that all else equal, foreign ministers with a diplomatic background have a lower chance of deposition than ministers without this type of background. The coefficient for this variable in Figure 11 is negative and highly statistically significant, which indicates that this type of experience reduces a minister's likelihood of forced resignation. However, our tests show that this variable has a nonproportional effect. To correct this, we have interacted the variable with the natural logarithm of a minister's tenure. The coefficient for this interaction *Diplomatic Experience*Ln(time)* is not statistically significant.

Thus, to fully capture the effect of *Diplomatic Experience* we need to add together these two estimates. This is a cumbersome operation. However, while there are several methods to interpret the substantive effects of nonproportional covariates (e.g., Licht 2011; Gandrud 2015), we can also visualize this effect in a graph. Figure 13 presents an estimate of the effect over time for *Diplomatic Experience* in a solid black line.[10] The 95 percent confidence interval is indicated by the dashed lines. The graph indicates that diplomatic experience only reduces a minister's likelihood of deposition up to year three approximately, where the bounds of the confidence interval are below zero. After that point in time, the estimate is indistinguishable from zero, which suggests that the effect of *Diplomatic Experience* disappears as tenure increases.

The evidence thus indicates that diplomatic experience only offers protection from deposition during early years in office. Indeed, foreign affairs might be a very complex portfolio and diplomatic experience may help with the initial part of the learning curve. But once the initial period in office has passed, previous diplomatic experience – regardless of how significant or extensive it was – may not determine the remaining tenure of a minister. For instance, French foreign ministers Edouard Thouvenel and Charles de La Valette, had extensive diplomatic experience but short tenure in office as ministers. Together, these individuals had accumulated multiple diplomatic posts before

---

[10] The technical term for this effect is the conditional linear coefficient of diplomatic experience.

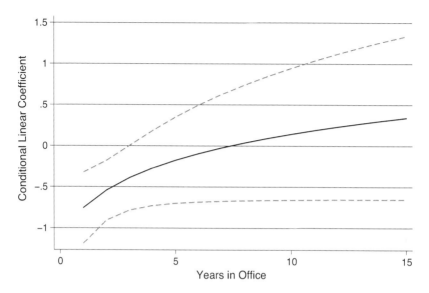

Figure 13 Effect of diplomatic experience in Model 2.

becoming Foreign Ministers, from Attachés and Chargé d'Affaires to Consuls and Ambassadors. Indeed, the Marquis de La Valette and Thouvenel had considerable diplomatic experience liaising with the Ottoman Empire around the time of the Crimean War, and yet they only managed to stay in office as foreign ministers for two and three years, respectively. This does not mean that diplomatic experience reduces tenure. Rather, it means that in the absence of diplomatic experience, and all else equal, these individuals would not have been in office for those periods of time, short as they may have been.

We follow the same technical procedure to explore the effect of *Military Experience* in Model 2. Specifically, Figure 14 indicates that military experience does not make a difference on a minister's chance of deposition early in their time in office, where the bounds of the confidence interval include zero. However, around year ten in office, the estimate becomes positive and significant, which indicates that ministers with longer tenure in office and military experience are more likely to be fired than ministers without this type of experience. However, it is important to note that this effect is only effective after the tenth year in office, which is well above the median tenure for ministers in our sample – only twelve individuals in our sample of ministers who have been forced out of office meet this condition.

For instance, only three foreign ministers with military experience and university education have been in office for ten years or longer: Zhou Enlain from China, Bernard von Bulow and Otto von Bismarck from Germany, have

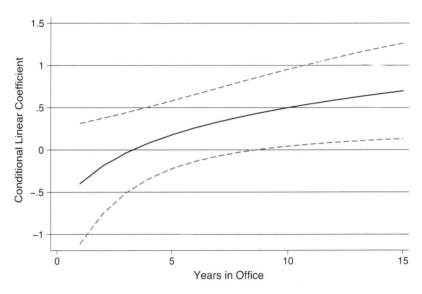

Figure 14 Effect of military experience in Model 2.

tenure of ten, thirteen, and twenty-nine years, respectively. In contrast, seven foreign ministers without military experience and university education have been in office for ten years or longer: Francis Osborne and William Grenville from the United Kingdom, Ludvig Manderström from Sweden, Maurice Couve de Murville from France, Agenor Goluchowski from Austria, Alberto Martin-Artajo from Spain, and Johan van Soelen from the Netherlands were in office for at least ten years. Altogether, military experience does not seem to determine the tenure of foreign ministers.

There are additional effects that are worth mentioning. For instance, a minister's education works in their favor and reduces their likelihood of deposition for periods of peace and for periods of peace and conflict. For this reason, the comparison of individual ministers with military experience mentioned earlier focuses on individuals with university education or above. Indeed, the estimate across Models 1 and 2 is consistently negative and significant, indicating that higher levels of education are associated with lower chances of deposition. However, this effect disappears for periods of international conflict.

In H3, we proposed that the initiation of disputes should increase the rate of ministerial deposition, as this may be interpreted as evidence of poor competence. The effect of the occurrence of a dispute can only be estimated in Model 2, the model that includes all observations in our sample. Model 2 shows that the variable *Any Dispute* is not statistically significant. This suggests that the occurrence of conflict does not determine the fate of foreign ministers. Quiroz

Flores (2016) argues that the effect of competence is mediated by political institutions – democratic leaders need competent ministers to deliver public goods, and therefore incompetence should increase the rate at which ministers lose office in democratic countries. A robustness test with an interaction of *Any Dispute* and *Polity Level of Democracy* shows that the occurrence of disputes continues to be insignificant. Results of these tests are available on our replication files.

The only conflict-related variable that seems to influence the rate of deposition is the number of MIDs that end in a particular year. Indeed, the variable *Number End Any MID* is negative and significant, suggesting that bringing conflicts to an end lowers the probability of dismissal for ministers that take part in the management of those disputes. This provides some validation of the idea that competence matters, although other relevant variables such as the outcomes of disputes continue to be insignificant.

To be sure of the effect of MID-related covariates, Model 3 restricts the sample to cases where the variable *Any Dispute* is equal to one. This is therefore a sample of periods of conflict. Estimates largely confirm previous results. First, it is worth noting that diplomatic and military experience do not break the proportionality assumption, and therefore they do not have to be corrected. In fact, the only troublesome variable in the model is political experience. This is therefore a simpler model to interpret.

Estimation results from Model 3 indicate that *Diplomatic Experience* reduces ministers' rates of deposition. Since the variable is proportional, this effect holds over the duration in office of ministers. This provides some validation to the effect of diplomatic experience discussed before, that is, protecting ministers for deposition during early years in office. In this model of conflict, the protection effect of diplomatic experience holds over the tenure of a minister. On the other hand, the effect of *Military Experience* in this model has now disappeared, which is generally in line with the results from Model 2, which indicated that military experience only had an effect on the tenure of ministers with long durations.

Lastly, the results confirm the negative effect of the number of disputes ended in a particular year; in other words, Model 3 also indicates that ending disputes reduces ministers' probability of dismissal. With the exception of the variable *Mean Dispute Level*, which is positive and significant, thus indicating that the severity of disputes increases the likelihood of deposition of ministers, all other conflict-related variables are indistinguishable from zero.

4.3 Conclusion

This section explains why some foreign ministers have longer tenure in office than others. Previous work has focused on principal-agent models to understand variation in ministerial tenure (e.g., Huber and Martinez-Gallardo 2008), while our own work has focused on the personal characteristics of ministers and their performance during conflict (Bäck et al. 2021). This section adds to this research agenda by using an updated database of foreign ministers and multiple-record data for ministerial tenure and the evolution of international disputes.

The analysis presented largely confirms our previous results. Our first hypothesis suggested that diplomatic experience should be associated with a lower probability of ministerial deposition. The evidence indicates that this is the case, although there are some interesting nuances. For instance, results from one model indicate that diplomatic experience only reduces a minister's chances of dismissal at the beginning of their post. However, a second model suggests the protective effect of diplomatic experience holds over the tenure of a minister. Altogether, it is safe to say that diplomatic experience lowers the probability of ministerial deposition, at least during early periods in office.

Our second hypothesis argued that military experience should also be associated with a lower probability of ministerial deposition. The evidence indicates that military experience generally does not determine tenure in office. One model indicates that a military background is not statistically significant and, at best, it increases the probability of deposition for a very small proportion of ministers, those with very long durations. However, evidence from another model strongly indicates that military experience is not statistically significant. Altogether, we can safely say that military experience does not have wide effects on the tenure of our sample of ministers.

Our third and fourth hypotheses focused on conflict-related performance and the likelihood of deposition. The evidence largely indicates that conflict in general does not make much difference in the tenure of foreign ministers. However, models indicate that bringing conflict to an end does reduce ministers' likelihood of deposition. This is a very interesting result. Indeed, it seems as if diplomatic experience reduces the probability of forced resignations. At the same time, it is very likely that diplomatic experience is manifested in ministers' ability to bring conflicts to an end. These two aspects of a minister's personal characteristics and abilities might help these types of individuals to stay longer in office. This also illuminates the result on military experience and conflict, which do not seem to determine tenure in office. In sum, the evidence in this section suggests that conflict-related performance may not be a key determinant of ministerial tenure, with personal characteristics and diplomatic ability playing a more important role.

This suggests that HoGs as principals evaluate the *ex ante* performance of potential ministers, looking at the individual background features of foreign ministers. The results are in line with the argument made by Quiroz Flores and Smith (2011), who argue that new ministers, by definition, have not revealed their level of performance – competence or performance, however defined or measured, is an unknown quantity. Yet, some ministers are more experienced than others, and the *expected* performance seems to keep ministers in office, at least until a sufficient quantity of actual performance is observed.

5 Conclusions

We have in this Element introduced an original dataset on the personal and professional background of foreign ministers, spanning thirteen countries and more than 200 years. We have used these data to answer three questions: who are the foreign ministers, why are foreign ministers with a particular background appointed to office, and why do some foreign ministers have longer tenure than others? To answer these questions, we started out this Element by presenting a theoretical framework for the study of foreign ministers as key political actors within the international system. We argued that the responsibilities of foreign ministers fall under three basic categories, with them being advisors, diplomats, and policy makers. In this chapter, we summarize our results and discuss the conclusions that can be drawn from our empirical analyses in terms of evaluating the expectations drawn from our theoretical framework.

Our theoretical expectations build on a principal-agent framework, conceiving of the relationship between the HoG and his or her foreign ministers as one of principal and agent. We suggested that HoGs will try to evaluate *ex ante* performance of potential ministers, which should be determined by the background features of foreign ministers, but they may also evaluate *ex post* performance, which is likely to be determined by situational features such as the level and outcomes of conflicts that the country is involved in. We centered specifically on foreign minister *experience* in our argument, with professional background as both the source of, and our measurement for, experience. Experience brings expertise, which have a variety of implications for decision-making and job performance. We highlighted three types of expertise in particular: diplomatic expertise, political expertise, and foreign policy expertise.

Our starting point of this entire project is that foreign ministers are key actors in international relations and in determining foreign policy outcomes – they are the actors who are officially appointed to direct foreign policy, and often have the discretion, institutional resources, authority, and legitimacy to shape foreign policy in a specific direction (see also Chrichlow 2005: 180). The question of whether foreign ministers actually have an impact on foreign policy outcomes is, however, not one we have studied in this Element. We believe that this is the next step for research in this field. In this final section we therefore also discuss important questions that can be analyzed using our data, focusing on foreign ministers' impact on some specific foreign policy outcomes.

5.1 Foreign Minister Background, Selection and Tenure

5.1.1 Why Are Foreign Ministers with a Particular Background Appointed?

Our historical data on foreign ministers shows that foreign ministers tend to have been men of politics, having had a career within the party or in legislative politics before appointment. They also show that their previous careers have typically not been within the military or diplomatic corps. However, the data also clearly shows that there is significant variation over time and across countries in the type of background that the foreign ministers have. We focused on explaining this variation in Section 3 of this Element, asking why foreign ministers with a particular background are appointed to office during certain times and in certain contexts.

Drawing on the principal-agent framework described in our theoretical section, we hypothesized that politicians with similar backgrounds to their HoGs (or state) are more likely to become foreign ministers, since HoGs expect that such ministers will have similar preferences to their own. For example, we expected that a HoG who has a military background is more likely to want to surround himself or herself with advisors, that is, foreign ministers, who have a background within the military. We also hypothesized that politicians who were experienced foreign policy makers, diplomats, or had a military background would be chosen to head the foreign office when the country faces an uncertain geopolitical situation since such ministers are likely to be expected to perform well under such circumstances.

All in all, the results are in line with our general expectations. First, we find that foreign ministers seem to be more likely to have military experience when the leader also has such a background, supporting the notion that leaders select ministers likely to share their preferences to minimize agency loss.

However, to fully evaluate such an argument we should ideally include information on the policy preferences of both leaders and individual politicians, since an individual's background is not a perfect predictor of his or her preferences. An analysis of legislative speeches made by politicians before their appointment to ministerial office could potentially be used to analyze the question of whether HoGs choose advisors with foreign policy preferences similar to their own, as has been done using more recent cabinet appointments in the United Kingdom and in some other Western European countries (see, e.g., Kam et al. 2010; Bäck et al. 2016). This is an important topic for future research.

We also find some support for the idea that contextual features matter for foreign minister selection. We find that foreign ministers were more likely to have a military background during the Cold War period, and to have previous experience as foreign minister during the Second World War and Cold War period, suggesting that policy expertise is important during times of uncertainty. We also find that foreign ministers are less likely to have a strong political background in autocracies, which supports the theoretical idea that individuals with such experience are perceived as potential challengers by autocratic leaders, who avoid promoting them to the important foreign policy office, which could strengthen such challengers' position.

To evaluate whether this is the mechanism underlying the effect of the democracy variable included in our selection analyses, it would be fruitful to also perform in-depth analyses of some specific cases, analyzing biographies and similar materials to get at the motivations of individual leaders.

5.1.2 Why Do Some Foreign Ministers Have Longer Tenure?

Our data presents considerable variation in the tenure in office of foreign ministers. Ministers have a median tenure of eight years. However, 25 percent of them have a tenure of less than three years, while another 25 percent stay in office for more than seventeen years. In trying to explain this variation, we focus on two sets of variables: personal characteristics of ministers related to their background and their performance in office during international conflict.

Like leaders, foreign ministers also provide public and private goods that secure the loyalty of political supporters (Bueno de Mesquita et al. 2003; Quiroz Flores 2016). Since foreign ministers are the highest diplomats in government, their provision of goods can be measured by the avoidance of military disputes by diplomatic means (Quiroz Flores 2016). In this Element we argue that this type of performance – and therefore tenure in office – is determined by the personal characteristics of ministers and the nature of military disputes. From a theoretical point of view, we expect that ministers' diplomatic and military experience are assets for a foreign minister and that they should be associated with a lower probability of deposition. Regardless of their background, we also expect that ministers who oversee the initiation of a dispute are more likely to be fired simply because they did not find a negotiated settlement. However, once a dispute has started, we also expect that victory would increase a minister's tenure in office.

We tested these theoretical expectations using survival analysis. The evidence is generally in line with our theoretical expectations, although with some very interesting nuances. For instance, we find that diplomatic experience provides protection from forced resignation only at the beginning of a term in office. In other words, and all else equal, ministers with diplomatic experience are relatively immune to deposition early in their term in office. Once they accumulate time in office, the effect of diplomatic experience disappears. Military experience, however, does not seem to have neither a negative nor a positive effect on tenure.

Theoretically, we think that the protective, yet short-lived effect of diplomatic experience and the null effect of military experience are confirmed by the evidence emerging from ministerial performance during disputes. Indeed, we find that the initiation and outcomes of military disputes do not determine a minister's survival in office. This is in line with the effect of military experience – this type of experience should be an asset in the decision to participate in a conflict and how to conduct it. However, neither of these factors determines ministerial tenure.

Nevertheless, the evidence indicates that bringing a conflict to an end does improve the prospects of staying in office. This is consistent with the effect of diplomatic experience. War and conflict are costly and putting a stop to bloodshed and destruction, sometimes even in the face of defeat, might be beneficial. Diplomacy has a crucial role in bringing conflict to an end, and we think that it is precisely at this point where a foreign minister with a diplomatic background might shine. Foreign ministers as top diplomats will certainly steer, and even directly participate in, peace talks. Therefore, diplomatic practice, sensibility, and understanding of negotiation processes and familiarity with the political position of contenders are incredibly important in conducting negotiations. This suggests that personal background and situational context may have an interactive effect: a diplomatic background provides protection from resignation, but it also contributes to successful peace talks and the likelihood of bringing conflict to an end, which also provides protection to ministers.

Altogether, we find that background and context have a key role in understanding tenure in office. However, the evidence indicates that the mechanisms behind the effect of these factors are complex and interactive. We hope that our new database will serve as a tool that will contribute to the development and testing of more nuanced hypotheses about ministerial tenure in office. At the same time, we hope to have raised questions about how to measure performance. Many countries do not face significant prospects for military conflict in international relations, such as in Latin America. In these cases, foreign ministers play a role in other areas, from international trade and participation in international organizations to migration, political integration, and the management of climate change. The logic behind our hypotheses can be extended to these areas, and our database will certainly be an asset in such future evaluations of the work of foreign ministers.

Further work may also elaborate on additional measures of competence for ministers of foreign affairs and how they interact with individual background and political institutions. In previous work (Bäck et al. 2021) we argued that the effect of a diplomatic background does not depend on political institutions – foreign ministers with diplomatic experience, who are likely to perform well, are not usually credible challengers to an autocrat, while the same competent ministers in democracies are kept in office due to good performance. Robustness tests from this section indicate that, indeed, interactions between dispute initiation – a measure of competence – and political institutions are not significant, thus validating our previous work. However, additional analyses may explore more nuanced tests of the interaction between institutions and performance in foreign affairs.

5.2 Are Foreign Ministers Advisors, Diplomats, or Policy Makers?

In the introductory section of this Element, we argued that the responsibilities of foreign ministers or secretaries of state fall under three basic categories. As *advisors*, foreign ministers occupy a key role as sources of information and arguments about the making of foreign policy. They make recommendations and provide expertise to leaders. As one of the highest-profile points of contact for foreign actors to the state, foreign ministers also serve a role as *diplomats*. In this capacity, they may negotiate treaties and manage crises. Lastly, as *policy makers*, foreign ministers often have significant authority in and of themselves to steer foreign policy in a certain direction, by making and enacting of foreign policy and diplomacy, which includes activities that range from crisis management to diplomatic recognition, to the administration of embassies.

Focusing on the questions of who is selected to be a foreign minister and who is allowed to remain in this office for a longer period of time, we have not explicitly analyzed which of these different roles foreign ministers take in their day-to-day work heading the foreign ministry. However, we can, based on our analyses of the background characteristics of who is appointed to lead the important foreign ministry, say something, at least indirectly, about which roles the foreign minister or secretary of state are expected to take.

One of the background characteristics of foreign ministers that we have stressed specifically in this Element is related to their diplomatic experience. We have done so since foreign ministers are often described as "the highest diplomats in government," representing "the sovereign state in one of its most important functions, that is, external relations" (Quiroz Flores 2009: 118). Are foreign ministers more likely to be experienced diplomats, and is there a variation across contexts when such experience matters more for who becomes and remains in the foreign ministry?

When analyzing our data spanning foreign minister appointments in thirteen former or current great powers over 200 years, we find, somewhat surprisingly, that foreign ministers overall have predominantly *not* had personal experience with diplomatic service abroad (Section 2). In countries such as Italy, the United Kingdom, and the United States, only some 20 percent of the foreign ministers have diplomatic background, whereas in countries such as Austria, China, France and Sweden, it is almost as common to have a foreign minister with as without diplomatic experience. Only in Russia, particularly during tsarist times, Prussia, and the Ottoman Empire, was diplomatic experience a modal feature among foreign ministers. We also see a clear trend over time, with a background in diplomacy being a much more common among foreign ministers appointed during the nineteenth century than it is today.

Analyzing whether diplomatic experience increases the tenure of foreign ministers (see Section 4), we find that diplomatic experience reduces a foreign minister's likelihood of forced resignation during a minister's early years in office. Hence, as an overall conclusion, diplomatic experience does seem to be important for foreign ministers, at least in certain contexts, especially more historical ones, and this type of background could also increase a foreign minister's expected performance in office, considering that it seems to insulate the minister from being fired from his or her position. This supports the idea that foreign ministers are diplomats, and that this is clearly one of the important roles for individuals heading the foreign ministry.

Some of our results instead speak to the advisory role of foreign ministers, in that leaders are likely to appoint foreign ministers with a background that is favorable in this role. In Section 3, focusing on the selection of foreign ministers, we analyzed whether leaders with military background were more likely to appoint foreign ministers with a similar military experience. Here, we find that a variable measuring the leader's combat experience is positive and significant, suggesting that leaders with considerable military experience are more likely to appoint foreign ministers with military experience. If our assumption is correct that individuals with a military background share similar foreign policy preferences, this suggests that leaders choose advisors whom they expect will implement policies that they themselves prefer.

Another result in our analyses of foreign minister selection that also supports the idea that foreign ministers are seen as important advisors to a leader is the one relating to the "complementarity" between leaders and ministers. Analyzing the selection of foreign ministers in Section 3, we find that the fewer years the prime minister or president has been in office, the more likely they are to appoint foreign ministers who have previously headed the foreign ministry. One reason for doing so is that a less experienced leader may need an experienced advisor to help him or her make competent foreign policy decisions. Hence, one important role of foreign ministers is clearly to be advisors to the leader.

Finally, some of our results signal that foreign ministers are also policy makers in their own right, supporting arguments made in the previous literature suggesting that foreign ministers have the discretion to influence foreign policy (Chrichlow 2005). In terms of political background, we have shown that foreign ministers are clearly no political outsiders. When counting membership in a political party or background in a legislature, in the cabinet, or other higher government office, only ten percent of the foreign ministers in our sample lack any such experience. In Section 2, we show that there is an overall trend in the appointment of foreign ministers, toward them becoming more and more political professionals. Since 1950, only a handful of foreign ministers in our entire sample have lacked political experience. The fact that having a political background is such an important feature attests to the policy making role of foreign ministers.

Our results with respect to foreign ministers in autocracies vis-à-vis democracies attest to the same point. Our interpretation of the finding that foreign ministers are less likely to have a strong political background in autocracies is that individuals with such experience are perceived as potential challengers by autocratic leaders, who avoid promoting them to the important foreign policy office, which could strengthen such challengers' position. Autocrats would, however, be unlikely to fear this competence of foreign ministers if their roles were restricted to that of diplomats and advisors. Foreign ministers are also policy makers.

5.3 The Impact of Foreign Ministers

While studying the consequences of who becomes foreign minister is beyond the scope of this Element, we will end with two illustrations of how our foreign minister data could be used in order to answer whether foreign ministers have an impact on foreign policy. It should be clear that these are only two suggestions, leaving out a range of possibilities for future research to consider.

5.3.1 Which Foreign Ministers Initiate and Escalate International Conflict?

One approach would be to analyze whether foreign minister background affects the escalation and outcome of international crises and disputes. Crises and disputes can end favorably or unfavorably, and some data exists that evaluates which way it did. Similarly, crises and disputes can escalate or not – some get worse, while others stabilize and then resolve. We have performed some preliminary analyses examining how the background of the foreign minister affects his or her ability to successfully manage and negotiate crises. In doing so, we examine the degree to which foreign minister experience affects one aspect of foreign minister performance, and the diplomatic success of the country they represent (von Hagen-Jamar and Bäck 2018).

In these analyses we draw on a dependent variable measuring whether there was a dispute or crisis onset in a given year, and a variable measuring whether there was an escalation of a dispute to violence in a given year. Here we make use of the MID dataset, which records each instance of a state threatening, displaying, or using military force against another state or states, and the International Crisis Behavior (ICB) dataset, which records instances of crises, defined as cases where the basic values of a state are threatened, with a finite amount of time to respond, and a high probability of military conflict. To specify these preliminary analyses, we relied heavily on the analyses presented by Shea and Poast (2018), who employ a Heckman selection model to control for the bias induced by only examining cases where a MID occurred in the second model (von Hagen-Jamar and Bäck 2018).

In our analyses, we found some support for a general expectation that experienced foreign ministers will make crises or disputes more frequent, in line with an idea that they will be more risk-acceptant than less experienced advisors. We predicted that foreign ministers with diplomatic experience will make escalation to violence less likely, assuming that they are better able to interpret signals sent by other states and may be better at advising the chief executive in achieving diplomatic outcomes. Here, we only found partial support for our hypothesis, with results showing that foreign ministers with diplomatic background experience lower rates of fatal disputes when making use of crisis data (ICB), but not when MID is used.

All in all, these preliminary results suggest that it is fruitful to connect our foreign minister data to datasets covering conflict datasets, and to analyze how the background of foreign ministers may influence foreign policy outcomes, for example, related to the initiation and escalation of conflict.

5.3.2 Does the Background of Foreign Ministers Matter for State Recognition?

Foreign ministers may clearly matter for a number of different types of foreign policy decisions and outcomes. One foreign policy decision that we have analyzed using our historical data on foreign ministers is state recognition. We have chosen to study state recognition because of its foundational role for the constitution of the international system and international society (Fabry 2010; Coggins 2014). States come into existence not only to the extent that they fulfill internal or domestic criteria of statehood, such as upholding a central government controlling its territory, but also, in order to function as states, they also need recognition from other states (e.g., Finer 1997; Jackson and Nexon 1999; Jönsson and Hall 2005). The question we ask, does the personal background characteristics of foreign ministers matter for which states are recognized?

In these preliminary analyses, we draw on Teorell (2023) in measuring state recognition through diplomatic representation. Simply put, a state is considered to recognize another state if it dispatches a diplomatic mission to another country at the level of chargé d'affaires or higher. Evidencing a causal relationship between personal characteristics of individual foreign ministers and foreign policy decisions on whether to recognize other states is clearly not a straightforward endeavor, and our empirical analyses focusing on this relationship are therefore only suggestive. Instead, we focus on investigating whether there is some evidence in support of plausible connections. Hence, we ask, does it seem to matter who was foreign minister at a particular time point for which states recognized which, even when structural characteristics of the countries and time period in question are taken into account (Teorell et al. 2018)?

One of the expectations we evaluate in this preliminary work relates to the diplomatic experience of foreign ministers. We expect prior diplomatic experience to be of importance for a foreign minister's likelihood to accept new members to the state system. Diplomatic background as such may not necessarily be linked to any particular preferences regarding the recognition of new states in general. However, personal experience with having been on a diplomatic mission *in a particular state* should make a foreign minister more likely to recognize that particular state.

Another expectation we present focuses on the regime type of the state under consideration for being recognized. Previous statistical studies of the late twentieth and early twenty-first centuries have found that regime similarity makes two countries more likely to exchange diplomatic missions (Duque 2018; Kinne 2014; Neumayer 2008). As pointed out by Osterhammel (2014: 579), monarchy was still in the late nineteenth century the modal form of government in the world, and although Fabry (2010) argues that "dynastic legitimism" was giving way to new principles of state legitimation, one could still expect that certain foreign ministers would be less likely to accept to inclusion of republics into the world order. More specifically, one could hypothesize that those from the "old elite" (or establishment) would be particularly unlikely to accept such novelty. We thus conjecture that noble foreign ministers are less (more) likely to recognize new states that are republics (monarchies).

Our hypotheses are evaluated statistically on a dyadic dataset of our thirteen current or former great powers (the recognizing parties) and a set of eighty-six states (the parties being recognized) that either came into existence or ceased to exist during the long nineteenth century (more specifically, from 1817–1914). While admittedly tentative, we find evidence for several systematic effects of background characteristics of the person most responsible for the conduct of foreign policy in a country. We find that foreign ministers with non-noble background are more likely to recognize new states that are republics than those that are monarchies; and foreign ministers are much more favorably disposed toward (re)recognizing countries from which they themselves have previous diplomatic experience (Teorell et al. 2018). Hence, the background of foreign ministers seems to matter for state recognition, supporting the idea these ministers do have an impact on important foreign policy outcomes.

Appendix

Table 7.1 Cox proportional hazards models of ministerial tenure

	Model 1	Model 2	Model 3
Previous term	0.36*	0.37**	0.43**
	(0.20)	(0.17)	(0.21)
Political experience	0.75	0.32**	-0.44
	(0.68)	(0.16)	(0.66)
Diplomatic experience	−1.05*	−1.12***	−0.37*
	(0.58)	(0.37)	(0.19)
Military experience	−1.3**	−0.77	0.16
	(0.51)	(0.51)	(0.25)
Gender	−0.55	−0.25	−0.55
	(10.6)	(10.3)	(0.90)
Age	0.00	0.00	0.00
	(0.00)	(0.00)	(0.00)
Head of Government	0.25	0.16	0.04
	(0.19)	(0.15)	(0.19)
Education	−0.2***	−0.13***	0.02
	(0.05)	(0.05)	(0.08)
Polity Level of democracy	−0.04***	−0.08***	−0.02
	(0.00)	(0.01)	(0.02)
Any dispute		−0.20	
		(0.16)	
Mean dispute level		−0.00	0.17***
		(0.11)	(0.05)
Number dispute win		0.09	−0.20
		(0.82)	(0.4)
Number dispute lose		−0.21	−0.17
		(10.1)	(0.6)
Number Start Any MID		−0.04	−0.07
		(0.07)	(0.09)
Number End Any MID		−0.38**	−0.37**
		(0.17)	(0.18)

Table 7.1 (cont.)

	Model 1	Model 2	Model 3
Ln(time)* Political experience	−0.35		0.82
	(0.43)		(0.64)
Ln(time)* Diplomatic experience	0.42	0.53*	
	(0.42)	(0.28)	
Ln(time)* Military experience	0.77**	0.53**	
	(0.32)	(0.24)	
Ln(time)* Gender	0.64	0.23	
	(0.83)	(0.8)	
Ln(time)* Polity Level of democracy		0.04***	
		(0.01)	
Ln(time)* Mean dispute level		0.13	
		(0.08)	
Ln(time)* Number dispute win		−0.27	
		(0.83)	
Ln(time)* Number dispute lose		−0.00	
		(0.8)	
Observations	1877	3329	1452
Subjects	745	1019	573
Failures	186	305	119
Log-likelihood	−989.4	−1792.5	−599.0

References

Alexiadou, Despina. 2016. *Ideologues, Partisans, and Loyalists: Ministers and Policymaking in Parliamentary Cabinets.* Oxford University Press.

Alexiadou, Despina, and Hakan Gunaydin. 2019. "Commitment or Expertise? Technocratic Appointments as Political Responses to Economic Crises." *European Journal of Political Research* 58(3): 845–865.

Anderson, Matthew Smith. 1993. *The Rise of Modern Diplomacy.* London & New York: Longman.

Bäck, Hanna, Marc Debus, and Wolfgang C. Müller. 2016. "Intra-party Diversity and Ministerial Selection in Coalition Governments." *Public Choice* 166: 355–378.

Bäck, Hanna, Jan Teorell, Alexander Von Hagen-Jamar, and Alejandro Quiroz Flores. 2021. "War, Performance and the Survival of Foreign Ministers." *Foreign Policy Analysis* 17(2): 1–12.

Box-Steffensmeier, Janet M., and Bradford S. Jones. 2004. *Event History Modelling: A Guide for Social Scientists.* Cambridge: Cambridge University Press.

Bueno de Mesquita, Bruce, and Randolph Siverson. 1995. "War and the Survival of Political Leaders: A Comparative Study of Regime Types and Political Accountability." *American Political Science Review* 89: 841–855.

Bueno de Mesquita, Bruce, Alastair Smith, Randolph M. Siverson, and James D. Morrow. 2003. *The Logic of Political Survival.* Cambridge, MA: MIT Press.

Buzan, Barry, and George Lawson. 2014. "Rethinking Benchmark Dates in International Relations." *European Journal of International Relations* 20(2): 437–462.

Byman, Daniel L., and Kenneth M. Pollack. 2001. "Let Us Now Praise Great Men: Bringing the Statesman Back In." *International Security* 25(4): 107–146.

Carlgren, Wilhelm. 1982. "Sweden: The Ministry of Foreign Affairs," in Steiner, Zara, ed. *The Times Survey of Foreign Ministries of the World.* London: Times Books, 455–470.

Chiozza, Giacomo, and Ajin Choi. 2003. "Guess Who Did What. Political Leaders and the Management of Territorial Disputes." *Journal of Conflict Resolution* 47(3): 251–278.

Chiozza, Giacomo, and Goemans, Hein. 2011. *Leaders and International Conflict.* Cambridge University Press.

Coggins, Bridget. 2014. *Power Politics and State Formation in the Twentieth Century: The Dynamics of Recognition*. Cambridge: Cambridge University Press

Crichlow, Scott. 2005. "Psychological Influences on the Policy Choices of Secretaries of State and Foreign Ministers." *Cooperation and Conflict: Journal of the Nordic International Studies Association* 40(2): 179–205.

Croco, Sarah and Jessica Weeks. 2016. "War Outcomes and Leader Tenure," *World Politics* 68(4), 577–607.

Cromwell, Valeries. 1982. "United Kingdom: The Foreign and Commonwealth Office," in Steiner, Zara, ed. *The Times Survey of Foreign Ministries of the World*. London: Times Books, 541–574.

Dallek, Robert. 2007. *Nixon and Kissinger: Partners in Power*. Harper Perennial.

De Santis, Hugh, and Waldo Heinrichs. 1982. "United States of America: The Department of State and American Foreign Policy," in Steiner, Zara, ed. *The Times Survey of Foreign Ministries of the World*. London: Times Books, 575–604.

Debs, Alexandre, and Goemans, Hein. 2010. "Regime Type, the Fate of Leaders, and War." *American Political Science Review* 104: 430–445.

Dethan, Georges. 1982. "France: The Ministry of Foreign Affairs since the Nineteenth Century," in Steiner, Zara, ed. *The Times Survey of Foreign Ministries of the World*. London: Times Books, 203–224.

Dewan, Torun, and Keith Dowding. 2005. "The Corrective Effect of Ministerial Resignations on Government Popularity." *American Journal of Political Science* 49(1): 46–56.

Doss, Kurt. 1982. "Germany: The History of the German Foreign Office," in Steiner, Zara, ed. *The Times Survey of Foreign Ministries of the World*. London: Times Books, 203–224.

Duque, Marina. 2018. "Recognizing International Status: A Relational Approach." *International Studies Quarterly* 62: 577–592.

Fabry, Mikulas. 2010. *Recognizing States: International Society & the Establishment of New States since 1776*. Oxford: Oxford University Press.

Fearon, James D. 1995. "Rationalist Explanations for War." *International Organization* 49(3): 379–414.

Finer, Samuel E. 1997. *The History of Government, I: Ancient Monarchies and Empires*. Oxford: Oxford University Press.

Gandrud, Christopher. 2015. "simPH: An R Package for Illustrating Estimates from Cox Proportional Hazard Models Including for Interactive and Nonlinear Effects." *Journal of Statistical Software* 65(i03): 1–20.

Goddard, Stacie E. 2009. "When Right Makes Might: How Prussia Overturned the European Balance of Power." *International Security* 33(3): 110–142.

Goemans, Henk E., Kristian Skrede Gleditsch, and Giacomo Chiozza. 2009. "Introducing Archigos: A Data Set of Political Leaders." *Journal of Peace Research* 46(2): 183–269.

Hagan, Joe D., Philip P. Everts, Haruhiro Fukui, and John D. Stempel. 2001. "Foreign Policy by Coalition: Deadlock, Compromise, and Anarchy." *International Studies Review* 3(2): 169–216.

Hallerberg, Mark, and Joachim Wehner. 2020. "When Do You Get Economists as Policy Makers?" *British Journal of Political Science* 50(3): 1193–1205.

Hermann, Margaret G. 1980. "Explaining Foreign Policy Behavior Using the Personal Characteristics of Political Leaders." *International Studies Quarterly* 24(1): 7–46.

Hermann, Margaret G. 2001. "How Decision Units Shape Foreign Policy: A Theoretical Framework." *International Studies Review* 3(2): 47–81.

Hermann, Margaret G., and Charles F. Hermann. 1989. "Who Makes Foreign Policy Decisions and How: An Empirical Inquiry." *International Studies Quarterly* 33(4): 361–387.

Hermann, Margaret G., and Thomas Preston. 1994. "Presidents, advisers, and foreign policy: The effect of leadership style on executive arrangements." *Political Psychology* 15(1): 75–96.

Hermann, Margaret G., and Joe D. Hagan. 1998. "International Decision Making: Leadership Matters." *Foreign Policy* 110: 124–137.

Holsti, Ole. 1970. "The 'Operational Code' Approach to the Study of Political Leaders: John Foster Dulles' Philosophical and Instrumental Beliefs." *Canadian Journal of Political Science/Revue canadienne de science politique* 3(1): 123–157.

Horowitz, Michael C., and Allan C. Stam. 2014. "How Prior Military Experience Influences the Future Militarized Behavior of Leaders." *International Organization* 68(3): 527–559.

Horowitz, Michael C., Stam, Allan, and Ellis, Cali 2015. *Why Leaders Fight*. Cambridge: Cambridge University Press.

Horowitz, Michael C., Phillip Potter, Todd S. Sechser, and Allan Stam. 2018. "Sizing Up the Adversary: Leader Attributes and Coercion in International Conflict." *Journal of Conflict Resolution* 62(10): 2180–2204.

Hsu, Immanuel. 1982. "The Development of the Chinese Foreign Office in the Ch'ing Period," in Steiner, Zara, ed. *The Times Survey of Foreign Ministries of the World*. London: Times Books, 119–134.

Indridason, Indridi, and Christopher Kam. 2008. "Cabinet Reshuffles and Ministerial Drift." *British Journal of Political Science* 38(4): 621–656.

Huber, John D., and Cecilia Martinez-Gallardo. 2008. "Replacing Cabinet Ministers: Patterns of Ministerial Stability in Parliamentary Democracies." *American Political Science Review* 102(2): 169–180.

Hudson, Valerie. 2005. "Foreign Policy Analysis: Actor Specific Theory and the Ground of International Relations." *Foreign Policy Analysis* 1: 1–30.

Jackson, Patrick Thaddeus, and Daniel Nexon. 1999. "Relations before States: Substance, Process, and the Study of World Politics." *European Journal of International Relations* 5(3): 291–333.

Jones, Benjamin T., and Shawna Metzger. 2019. "Different Words, Same Song: Advice for Substantively Interpreting Duration Models." *PS: Political Science & Politics* 52(4): 691–695.

Jönsson, Christer and Martin Hall. 2005. *Essence of Diplomacy*. London: Palgrave Macmillan.

Kaarbo, Juliet, and Margaret G. Hermann. 1998. "Leadership Styles of Prime Ministers: How Individual Differences Affect the Foreign Policymaking Process." *The Leadership Quarterly* 9(3): 243–263.

Kam, Christopher, and Indridi H. Indridason. 2005. "The Timing of Cabinet Reshuffles in Five Westminster Parliamentary Systems." *Legislative Studies Quarterly* 30(3): 327–363.

Kam, Christopher, William T. Bianco, Itai Sened, and Regina Smyth. 2010. Ministerial selection and intraparty organization in the contemporary British parliament. *American Political Science Review* 104(2), 289–306.

Keele, Luke. 2010. "Proportionally Difficult: Testing for Nonproportional Hazards in Cox Models." *Political Analysis* 18(2): 189–205.

Kinne, Brandon J. 2014. "Dependent Diplomacy: Signaling, Strategy, and Prestige in the Diplomatic Network." *International Studies Quarterly* 58: 247–259.

Kissinger, Henry A. 1994. *Diplomacy*. New York: Simon & Schuster.

Kowert, Paul A., and Margaret G. Hermann. 1997. "Who Takes Risks? Daring and Caution in Foreign Policy Making." *Journal of Conflict Resolution* 41(5): 611–637.

Krcmaric, Daniel, Stephen C. Nelson, and Andrew Roberts. 2020. "Studying Leaders and Elites: The Personal Biography Approach." *Annual Review of Political Science* 23(1): 133–151.

Kuneralp, Sinan. 1982. "Turkey: The Ministry of Foreign Affairs under the Ottoman Empire and the Turkish Republic," in Steiner, Zara, ed. *The Times Survey of Foreign Ministries of the World*. London: Times Books, 493–514.

Leira, Halvard. 2019. "The Emergence of Foreign Policy." *International Studies Quarterly* 63: 187–198.

Levy, Jack. 1983. *War in the Modern Great Power System, 1495–1975.* Lexington: University Press of Kentucky.

Licht, Amanda A. 2011. "Change Comes with Time: Substantive Interpretation of Nonproportional Hazards in Event History Analysis." *Political Analysis* 19(2): 227–243.

Markowitz, Jonathan N., and Christopher J. Fariss. 2018. "Power, proximity, and democracy: Geopolitical competition in the international system." *Journal of Peace Research* 55(1): 78–93.

Mitzen, Jennifer. 2005. "Reading Habermas in Anarchy: Multilateral Diplomacy and Global Public Spheres." *American Political Science Review* 99(3): 401–417.

Modelski, George. 1970. "The World's Foreign Ministers: A Political Elite." *Journal of Conflict Resolution* 14(2): 135–175.

Morrow, James D. 1989. "Capabilities, Uncertainty, and Resolve: A Limited Information Model of Crisis Bargaining." *American Journal of Political Science* 33(4): 941–972.

Neto, Octavio Amorim, and Kaare Strøm. 2006. "Breaking the Parliamentary Chain of Delegation: Presidents and Non-partisan Cabinet Members in European Democracies." *British Journal of Political Science* 36(4): 619–643.

Neumann, Iver B. 2012. *At Home with the Diplomats.* Ithaca: Cornell University Press.

Neumayer, Eric. 2008. "Distance, Power and Ideology: Diplomatic Representation in a World of Nationstates." *Area* 40(2): 228–236.

Nicolson, Harold. 1939. *Diplomacy.* London: Thornton Butterworth.

Nish, Ian. 1982. "Japan: The Foreign Ministry," in Steiner, Zara, ed. *The Times Survey of Foreign Ministries of the World.* London: Times Books, 327–344.

Osterhammel, Jürgen. 2014. *The Transformation of the World: A Global History of the Nineteenth Century.* Princeton: Princeton University Press.

Palmer, Glenn, Vito D'Orazio, Michael Kenwick, and Matthew Lane. 2015. "The MID4 Data Set: Procedures, Coding Rules, and Description." *Conflict Management and Peace Science* 32(2): 222–242.

Park, Sunhee, and David J. Hendry. 2015. "Reassessing Schoenfeld Residual Tests of Proportional Hazards in Political Science Event History Analyses." *American Journal of Political Science* 59(4): 1072–1087.

Preston, Thomas. 2001. *The President and His Inner Circle: Leadership Style and the Advisory Process in Foreign Policy Making.* New York: Columbia University Press.

Quiroz Flores, Alejandro. 2009. "The Political Survival of Foreign Ministers." *Foreign Policy Analysis* 5(2): 117–133.

Quiroz Flores, Alejandro. 2016. *Ministerial Survival During Political and Cabinet Change. Foreign Affairs, Diplomacy and War.* London: Routledge.

Quiroz Flores, Alejandro. 2022. *Survival Analysis: A New Guide for Social Scientists.* Elements Series in Quantitative and Computational Methods. Cambridge University Press. In Press.

Quiroz Flores, Alejandro, and Alastair Smith. 2011. "Leader Survival and Cabinet Change." *Economics and Politics* 23(3): 345–366.

Risse, Thomas. 2000. "'Let's Argue!': Communicative Action in World Politics." *International Organization* 54(1): 1–39.

Rumpler, Helmut. 1982. "Austria: The Foreign Ministry of Austria and Austria-Hungary 1848 to 1918," in Steiner, Zara, ed. *The Times Survey of Foreign Ministries of the World.* London: Times Books, 33–48.

Satow, Ernest Mason. 1922. *A Guide to Diplomatic Practice: Vol. 1.* London: Longmans.

Saunders, Elizabeth N. 2017. "No Substitute for Experience: Presidents, Advisers, and Information in Group Decision Making." *International Organization* 71(S1): S219–S247.

Serra, Enrico. 1982. "Italy: The Ministry of Foreign Affairs," in Steiner, Zara, ed. *The Times Survey of Foreign Ministries of the World.* London: Times Books, 297–326.

Sharp, Paul. 1999. "For Diplomacy: Representation and the Study of International Relations." *International Studies Review* 1(1): 33–57.

Shea, Patrick E., and Paul Poast. 2018. "War and Default." *Journal of Conflict Resolution* 62(9): 1876–1904.

Smyth, Denis. 1982. "Spain: Spain's First Secretariat of State, Ministry of State and Ministry of Foreign Affairs," in Steiner, Zara, ed. *The Times Survey of Foreign Ministries of the World.* London: Times Books, 423–454.

Strøm, Kaare. 2003. "Parliamentary Democracy and Delegation" in K. Strøm, W. C. Muller, and T. Bergman, eds. *Delegation and Accountability in Parliamentary Democracies.* Oxford: Oxford University Press, 55–108.

Svolik, Milan. 2012. *The Politics of Authoritarian Rule.* Cambridge: Cambridge University Press.

Teorell, Jan, Hanna Bäck and Alexander von Hagen-Jamar. 2018. "Foreign Ministers and State Recognition in the Long 19th Century," Unpublished paper. Department of Political Science, Lund University.

Teorell, Jan. 2023. "Rules of Recognition? Explaining Diplomatic Representation since the Congress of Vienna." *Cooperation and Conflict* 58(2): 155–174.

Teorell, Jan, Michael Coppedge, Staffan Lindberg and Svend-Erik Skaaning. 2019. "Measuring Polyarchy across the Globe, 1900–2017," *Studies in Comparative International Development* 54(1): 71–95.

Trager, Robert F. 2010. "Diplomatic Calculus in Anarchy: How Communication Matters." *American Political Science Review* 104(2): 347–368.

Trager, Robert F. 2016. "The Diplomacy of War and Peace." *Annual Review of Political Science* 19(1): 205–228.

Uldricks, Teddy. 1982. "Union of Soviet Socialist Republics: The Tsarist and Soviet Ministry of Foreign Affairs," in Steiner, Zara, ed. *The Times Survey of Foreign Ministries of the World*. London: Times Books, 513–540.

von Hagen-Jamar, Alexander., and Hanna Bäck. 2018. "Politicians, Soldiers and Diplomats: A Comparative Analysis of Foreign Minister Experience and the Initiation and Escalation of International Disputes." Unpublished manuscript, Lund: Lund University

Wels, Cornelis B. 1982. "Netherlands: The Foreign Policy Institutions in the Dutch Republic and the Kingdom of the Netherlands," in Steiner, Zara, ed. *The Times Survey of Foreign Ministries of the World*. London: Times Books, 363–390.

Wu, Cathy Xuanxuan, and Wolford, Scott. 2018. "Leaders, States, and Reputations." *Journal of Conflict Resolution* :62(10): 2087–2117.

Acknowledgments

This Element is a product of a research program, "State-Making and the Origins of Global Order in the Long Nineteenth Century and Beyond", which was held at the Department of Political Science at Lund University. We are very grateful to the participants of this research program who have given us constructive and helpful feedback on drafts of texts that have become part of this Element. We are especially indebted to Alexander von Hagen-Jamar who was part of this project on foreign ministers from the start, and who has made invaluable contributions to this Element. The program was generously funded by *Riksbankens Jubileumsfond* (M14-0087:1).

We also want to thank all of those people who were involved in collecting the historical data on the background and exit reasons of foreign ministers and secretaries of state in the countries analyzed in this Element. More specifically, we are grateful to Erik Meier for his help in creating the dataset on Austria and Germany, to Martin Hansen for compiling and complementing the final dataset, and for the excellent research assistance provided by Lina Hjärtström (United Kingdom, United States, and Sweden), Emanuel Hübner (Germany), Justus Kalthoff (Austria), Bernardo Isola (Italy), Selin Altindis (Ottoman Empire), Cem Mert Dalli (Turkey), Josje Groustra (Netherlands), Marina Polinovskaya (Russia), Pia Lonnakko (France), Francesco Ferrer Martinez (Spain), Susumu Annaka (Japan), and Sun Qi (China).

Alejandro Quiroz Flores would like to acknowledge the support of the Business and Local Government Data Research Centre (ES/S007156/1) funded by the Economic and Social Research Council (ESRC) for undertaking this work. https://esrc.ukri.org The funding body did not play a role in study design, data collection, analysis, decision to publish, or preparation of the manuscript.

Cambridge Elements ⌐

International Relations

Series Editors

Jon C. W. Pevehouse
University of Wisconsin–Madison

Jon C. W. Pevehouse is the Mary Herman Rubinstein Professor of Political Science and Public Policy at the University of Wisconsin–Madison. He has published numerous books and articles in IR in the fields of international political economy, international organizations, foreign policy analysis, and political methodology. He is a former editor of the leading IR field journal, International Organization.

Tanja A. Börzel
Freie Universität Berlin

Tanja A. Börzel is the Professor of political science and holds the Chair for European Integration at the Otto-Suhr-Institute for Political Science, Freie Universität Berlin. She holds a PhD from the European University Institute, Florence, Italy. She is coordinator of the Research College "The Transformative Power of Europe," as well as the FP7-Collaborative Project "Maximizing the Enlargement Capacity of the European Union" and the H2020 Collaborative Project "The EU and Eastern Partnership Countries: An Inside-Out Analysis and Strategic Assessment." She directs the Jean Monnet Center of Excellence "Europe and its Citizens."

Edward D. Mansfield
University of Pennsylvania

Edward D. Mansfield is the Hum Rosen Professor of Political Science, University of Pennsylvania. He has published well over 100 books and articles in the area of international political economy, international security, and international organizations. He is Director of the Christopher H. Browne Center for International Politics at the University of Pennsylvania and former program co-chair of the American Political Science Association.

Editorial Team

International Relations Theory

Jeffrey T. Checkel, European University Institute, Florence

International Security

Anna Leander, Graduate Institute Geneva

International Political Economy

Edward D. Mansfield, University of Pennsylvania

Stafanie Walter, University of Zurich

International Organisations

Tanja A. Börzel, Freie Universität Berlin

Jon C. W. Pevehouse, University of Wisconsin–Madison

About the series

The Cambridge Elements Series in International Relations publishes original research on key topics in the field. The series includes manuscripts addressing international security, international political economy, international organizations, and international relations.

Cambridge Elements ⁼

International Relations

Elements in the series

A full series listing is available at: www.cambridge.org/EIR

Printed in the United States
by Baker & Taylor Publisher Services